PLATO'S INSIGHT

How Physical Exercise Boosts Mental Excellence

CHONG CHEN, PH.D.

Brain & Life Publishing

London

With education and exercise, man can attain perfection.

— Plato

ALSO BY CHONG CHEN

*Fitness Powered Brains: Optimize Your Productivity, Leadership
And Performance*

ISBN 978-1-9997601-1-3 Ebook

ISBN 978-1-9997601-2-0 Paperback

Brain & Life Publishing

27 Old Gloucester Street, London, U.K.

Printed in the United Kingdom. First Printing, 2017

For information about special needs for bulk purchases, sales promotions, and educational needs, please contact orders@brainandlife.net.

To my parents for their love and support

TABLE OF CONTENTS

CHAPTER 1
Plato's Insight

Imagine this. You are taking a shuttle run test in high school. "Good morning!" the teacher says, "today we are going to do some running, this is not a race, but we want to see how long you can run. You only have to run back and forth across the 20-meter space. The running will be easier in the beginning but progressively get more challenging."

Following the rules, at the sound of the beep, you run to the other end of the 20-meter space and stand behind the line. When you hear the beep again, you run back to the opposite side and wait behind that other line. When you hear a triple beep, the pace quickens, and you must run faster before the beep sounds again. If you fail to reach the line by the time the beep sounds, you get a "miss." After two misses, you'll be scored on your best performance.

A rather simple running test, isn't it? This shuttle running test is the Progressive Aerobic Cardiovascular Endurance Run (PACER). PACER was created by two Canadian sports scientists in 1982. It is now used worldwide to assess aerobic capacity in children, adolescents, and adults. As we increase our effort during exercise, the oxygen we consume to produce energy increases.

However, there is a maximum level of oxygen consumption which determines our endurance during prolonged exercise. This level of oxygen consumption is called maximal oxygen consumption, or VO_2 max. It reflects the aerobic capacity or fitness level of an individual. In the PACER test, students run back and forth across the 20-meter space at a pace that gets faster each minute. The amount of oxygen they consume subsequently increases and eventually approaches the VO_2 max. Thus, a student's score on the PACER test can be an indicator of his or her aerobic fitness level.

Psychologists Arthur Kramer, Charles Hillman and their colleagues at the University of Illinois at Urbana-Champaign, administered the PACER test to hundreds of elementary school students. Then they did something extraordinary. They looked at the association between the students' PACER scores and their academic performance in math and reading. As a result, the students' PACER score turned out to be a rather good predictor of their academic performance. The higher the PACER score, the higher their scores in math and reading on standardized tests. As PACER score reflects aerobic fitness, this finding suggests that higher levels of aerobic fitness are associated with better academic achievement.

But how significant is this association? In this study, aerobic fitness explains approximately 23.2% and 16% of the individual difference (statistically called variance) in the scores of math and reading, respectively. In another famous study by Angela Duckworth and Martin Seligman (the father of positive psychology) at the University of Pennsylvania, general intelligence, as measured by a standard IQ test, explains just 10.2% of the individual difference in overall academic achievement, including math and reading. Put it differently, aerobic fitness is more important than intelligence.

Why?

Many factors affect academic achievement, and intelligence is one. Aerobic fitness boosts most, if not all, of the factors essential for academic achievement, including intelligence. That's why fitness beats intelligence. Impressive.

Physical activity, or exercise (below we use them interchangeably), is a key to building fitness. People that regularly engage in physical activity generally have higher levels of fitness. Thus, the above finding highlights the potential benefits of physical activity. More than two thousand years ago, the Greek philosopher Plato said, *"In order for man to succeed in life, God provided him with two means, education and physical activity. Not separately, one for the soul and the other for the body, but for the two together. With these two means, man can attain perfection."* I never understood what Plato meant by this sentence until I came across the above study. For the first time, it hit me that physical activity builds not only man's body, but also his soul (i.e. mind and brain). Physical exercise boosts mental excellence. It was the above evidence and insight that led me to the field of the neurobiology of exercise where I opened my doctorate dissertation at Hokkaido University. It was also the above evidence and insight that inspired me to go beyond my own research and ask how exercise benefits our ability to think and learn, and what kind of exercise brings the greatest benefits. The result is this book. Enjoy.

~~~

CHAPTER 2
Physically Active Students Perform Better at School

I have always been deeply moved by outstanding achievement and saddened by wasted potential.

— Stanford Psychologist Carol Dweck

In my elementary, junior and senior high school, all the students had to attend a daily 30-minute running session in the early morning. We were also required to participate in a 30-minute radio calisthenics every day during the morning recess. At that time, the benefits of exercise on our minds and brains never came to me. I was told that attending these physical activities would prevent me from catching a cold and earn us prizes at physical and calisthenics competitions. Neither did my classmates know the benefits. They thought attending these activities was a waste of time and did no good to their studies. Many kept skipping the running and radio calisthenics sessions using every kind of excuses. They secretly studied in the classroom instead while others were exercising.

Physical Education or Academic Instruction?

Parents, teachers, school officers, and governmental policy makers have similar concerns. School and afterschool time are too important for better academic achievement to be wasted on physical education (PE) and exercise. Take America for example, in response to budget concerns and pressures to improve academic test scores, many states and schools have downsized or eliminated PE from the school curriculum. But does reducing time for PE improve academic performance? Does increasing time for PE decrease academic achievement?

The scientific community has been asking the same questions. Decades of research have provided concrete evidence that the popular assumption that PE conflicts with students' learning is not true. A 2003 survey of over 500 American elementary schools shows that decreasing or eliminating the time for PE, music, and art and using that time for main subjects (for example, math and reading) did not increase students' performance on those main subjects. In contrast, increasing the time for PE in the curriculum improves academic achievement. In a study of over 300 American 4th-grade students, compared to those who received 28 hours of PE per school year, those with 56 or more hours of PE per school year scored higher on tests of English and language arts. Assuming 32 weeks a year, it means students who had 105 minutes or more per week of PE performed better than those who had only 52.5 minutes per week of PE. In another Canadian study, scientists modified the curriculum of over 500 1st grade elementary students, so an additional hour per day of PE was scheduled after the daily instruction. Control students in the same school took the traditional curriculum and received an additional hour per day of academic instruction when students in the experimental group were doing exercise. That curriculum was maintained through the following six years. Annual school tests showed that, although students in the experimental group had somewhat lower grades in the 1st grade, they outperformed their schoolmates from the 2nd through the 6th grade in French, math, English, and natural science. Although with 13-14% less school time spent on academic instruction, these students learned more. Increasing time for PE pays off.

Physically Active Students Get Higher Marks at School

It is now evident that physically active students perform better at school compared to the less active students. Several national health surveys in Australia, Hong Kong, Iceland, the U.K. and the U.S. have provided compelling evidence. For instance, one Australian study of nearly 8,000 7-15 years old children reported that the more physical activity during morning recess and lunchtime a child engaged in, the higher academic scores he/she achieved. Thus, instead of mind wandering, playing smartphone games, or doing homework during the breaks, those walking or running around, playing sports or physically engaging games eventually got better performances in various subjects.

Another American national study analyzed data from nearly 12,000 high school students. Relative to those who frequently watched television or videos, those who regularly participated in school-based physical activities (including team and individual sports, academic clubs) or played sports with their parents were over 20 percent more likely to earn an A in math and English. Meanwhile, the physically active students smoked less, showed less truancy without an excuse, and did more work for pay outside of the home and during summer, and did more housework. Those who played sports with their parents further showed reduced violent behaviors, less drinking, less use of illegal drugs, increased seatbelt usage, and were more likely to get enough sleep each night. As we will see in

Chapter 10, parenting and the parent-child relationship plays a significant role in children's cognitive, emotional, and social development. Playing sports with parents increases children's communication with their parents and promotes optimal development.

Notably, the benefits of exercise on academic achievement have been quantified by meta-analysis. Scientists use meta-analysis to combine data from a large number of studies and identify a common effect size. The effect size reflects to what extent a particular intervention (e.g., exercise) causally changes the target outcome (e.g., academic achievement).

So far, scientists have performed two meta-analyses quantifying to what extent regular exercise and high fitness levels benefit academic performance. In a 2003 meta-analysis, Benjamin Sibley and Jennifer Etnier at Arizona State University reported an overall effect size of 0.30. As for the particular benefit on math, the effect size is 0.20. In another 2011 meta-analysis, Alicia Fedewa and Soyeon Ahn at the University of Kentucky reported an overall effect size of 0.27. As for the particular benefit on math and reading, the effect sizes were 0.44 and 0.36, respectively.

How significant are effect sizes of this magnitude? I will give you two examples. First, in the past 20 years, it has frequently been reported that various music training programs such as keyboard or voice lessons enhance children's reading skills. A 2008 meta-analysis quantified this benefit and reported an effect size of 0.32. As in the above 2011 meta-analysis, the effect size of physical activity or fitness on reading achievement is 0.36. The benefit of exercise is substantial. Second, effect sizes of this magnitude transform into considerable academic scores. One study compared children at the highest and lowest quantiles of aerobic fitness. The difference in their math and reading scores was approximately 15% points on standardized tests. Unbelievable! (Still, after reading this book, you will find it easily understandable.)

The scientific evidence depicts a correlation between physical activity and academic performance. It repeatedly reinforces the idea that regularly engaging in exercise promotes academic achievement. The reasons are multifold. First, exercise improves executive function (a core set of cognitive abilities, see Chapter 3) and memory (Chapter 4). It thus promotes the efficiency of learning. Second, exercise increases people's capacity for self-regulation or self-discipline. Self-discipline determines how much effort a student spends on learning and is more important than IQ in regards to affecting academic achievement (Chapter 7). Third, exercise boosts positive moods (Chapter 5), buffers stress (Chapter 6), reduces negative moods (Chapter 8), and improves sleep quality (Chapter 9). And the net result is enhanced academic performance.

What Kind of Exercise Brings the Most Benefit?

Two pieces of good news are important for you to know. First, every child, including those overweight (see Chapter 12), can benefit from increasing physical activity and fitness. Genetic research shows that the association between aerobic fitness and intelligence is primarily explained by the modifiable environment ($\geq 80\%$), whereas the unchangeable heritability explains $<15\%$ of the association. It suggests that everyone can considerably benefit (e.g., improve intelligence) from increasing aerobic fitness by modifying his/her environment (i.e., participating in exercise). Second, as shown in the subsequent chapters, physical activity and fitness is not only beneficial for children and adolescents but also adults and older people.

So what kind of exercise brings the most benefit? Here is the answer:

●　　As least 20 minutes of exercise may be necessary for the cognition-enhancing effect to occur.

●　　The greatest effects on academic achievement occur when children engage in aerobic exercise, like running, jogging, playing soccer, rather than resistance or strength training activities, like push-ups or sit-ups.

●　　Vigorous- or moderate-intensity exercise, like running and playing tag, have effects larger than low-intensity exercise such as walking.

●　　Cognitive-challenging exercise requiring more strategies and physical coordination (e.g., balancing, reacting, adjusting, and differentiating), such as soccer, tennis, and volleyball, is associated with better concentration on academic tasks.

●　　Doing exercise in small (less than 10 people) or medium (10-30 people) groups brings greater benefit than in large groups (30 or more people) or doing exercise alone.

●　　Engaging in exercise in a mixed-gender group brings greater benefit than in a single-gender group.

●　　The greatest cognitive benefits from physical education occur when the physical education classes are scheduled during the early or middle part of the day, compared to at the end of the day. It is because the benefit of exercise on learning efficiency peaks within tens of minutes following an exercise session and then gradually decays. This benefit is better reflected when giving children time to study.

Most People Are Physically Inactive

Here I want to make my point more straightforward to help you better understand the benefit of exercise. It is true that exercise promotes academic achievement. Yet, it doesn't mean a student who exercises more will always outperform another who works out less. Effort and many other factors count as well. But given the same effort, those who exercise more will have a better chance at achieving more. For a certain student, the more he/she exercises, the more benefits he/she gets. For the latter point, strictly speaking, it is only true within a certain amount of exercise. That is, there is a tradeoff between the increased learning efficiency and the lost time studying. If you spend all your time playing sports without hitting the books and listening to lectures, I can't promise you a high score in math or reading. Yet, scientists haven't provided evidence that exercise has a negative impact on achievement. Partly, it is because most students and regular people are physically inactive (see below). Thus, at this moment, we need not worry about exercising too much. What we should worry about is whether or not we have exercised enough.

For the general population, in order to attain an optimal level of health for the body and brain, various national or international guidelines suggest at least weekly 150 minutes of moderate- or 75 minutes of vigorous-intensity exercise. While doing moderate-intensity exercise, we should be able to talk but unable to sing. Examples are brisk walking, double tennis, table tennis, gardening, and ballroom dancing. While doing vigorous-intensity exercise, we cannot talk without pausing for breath. Examples are jogging, single tennis, swimming laps, and jumping rope.

Despite the recommendations, over 60-70% of people in many countries, including China, Japan, the U.K., and U.S., fail to engage in this amount of exercise and remain sedentary or physically inactive. Recently, the Committee on Physical Activity and Physical Education in the School Environment Institute of Medicine of the U.S., recognized that attaining a daily 60 minutes of moderate to vigorous-intensity exercise is essential for optimal learning in the classroom for children and adolescents. This recommendation is robustly evidence-based. However, the reality is upsetting: up to 80% students fail to achieve this goal. If you're one inactive person or student, I invite you to start exercising seriously. As you'll see in later chapters, it will benefit you in almost every aspect of your daily life.

~_~

CHAPTER 3
Playing Tennis for Just 50 Minutes Improves Executive Function

When you read a book, the neurons in your brain fire overtime, deciding what the characters are wearing, how they're standing, and what it feels like the first time they kiss. No one shows you. The words make suggestions. Your brain paints the pictures.

— American writer, Meg Rosoff

I came across the aerobic-fitness-explains-23.2%-of-math-achievement study when I was a first-year graduate student at Hokkaido University. Back then I was attending a seminar held by Professor Masao Mizuno in his Physical Fitness Lab. Professor Mizuno had just established his lab for five years. Before that, he spent 26 years in Denmark researching physical fitness science. He had been interested in how exercise influences cognition and mental health. One of his Ph.D. students, Toru Ishihara, picked up the topic of how exercise affects cognitive function. Ishihara made an exciting find that playing tennis for just 50 minutes improved executive function. We previously said cognitive-challenging activities provide more benefits to academic achievement. Tennis is one typical example of such activities. However, before we introduce Ishihara's research, let's get familiar with the concept of executive function.

What Is Executive Function and Why Is It Important?

Modern psychological theories of cognitive ability typically include an executive component. The executive component coordinates goal-directed behavior by controlling attention. It is this executive component that essentially determines fluid intelligence (FI), one of two types of general intelligence.

FI is the ability to solve novel, abstract problems. These problems need mental operations that make little use of the real world information. The other type of general intelligence is crystallized intelligence (CI). CI is stored information about the world and learned procedures that help you to make inferences about it. Whereas FI is reasoning and problem-solving skills, CI is the general knowledge. In everyday life, we describe people with high FI as smart, while describing people with high CI as wise. For instance, during the aging process, FI shows a gradual decline while CI remains relatively unaffected until a later age. That is why we often say older people harvest wisdom.

FI is determined by the executive component. Neuropsychologists call this executive component "executive function." Executive function consists of three parts, inhibitory control, cognitive flexibility, and working memory. We will explain each of these functions in Ishihara's research.

How Playing Tennis Improves Executive Function

Ishihara studied the effects of a 50-minute tennis lesson in elementary school students. Before and after the lesson, he administered three tests evaluating three independent parts of executive function. His findings were this: compared to before the lesson, the students showed an enhanced executive function following the lesson.

The first part of executive function is inhibitory control. It is the process of suppressing a goal-inconsistent response. Here, inhibitory control was measured by the Stroop Color-Word Test (or the Stroop Test). In this test, a word indicating a particular color and the color of the word were incongruently presented. For instance, the word "RED" was printed in green and "GREEN" in blue. Subjects had to quickly indicate the color of the word while ignoring the meaning of the word. A rather simple test, but it captured a fundamental cognitive process. In general, people find it easier to read the word as written directly and harder to name the color of the word. Subjects had to suppress the temptation to respond to the meaning of the word. The speed and accuracy of a subject's response reflected their capacity for inhibitory control. Compared to baseline, after a 50-minute tennis lesson, the students were faster at naming the incongruent color of the word, suggesting enhanced inhibitory control ability.

The second part of executive function is cognitive flexibility. Cognitive flexibility refers to the mental ability to switch between thinking in different dimensions and levels, and thinking about different concepts. Ishihara evaluated cognitive flexibility using the Local-Global Task. In this task (see figure below), a geometric figure comprising a "global" number (1, 2, 3, or 4) composed of smaller, "local" numbers (1, 2, 3, or 4) was randomly presented. Numbers 1 and 2 were the target numbers and were equally likely to occur at the global and local levels. In contrast, numbers 3 and 4 were distracters appearing at the opposite level of the target numbers. Children had to indicate whether a target number (1 or 2) was at the global or local level fast. For instance, in the first trial of the following figure, the target number 2 was at the global level. The level of the target number was alternated and the reaction time following the alternation, namely to indicate the level of the new target number, represents cognitive flexibility.

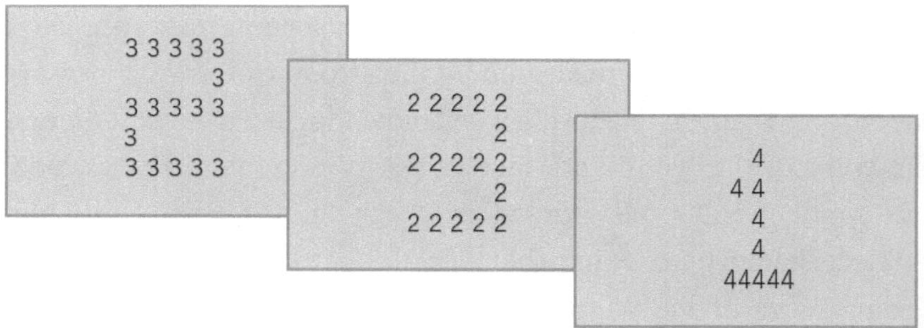

Ishihara found that the 50-minute tennis lesson enhanced children's performance on the Local-Global Task. They were much faster at indicating whether the target number was at the global or local level after the lesson, suggesting enhanced cognitive flexibility.

The third part of executive function is working memory. Working memory is perhaps best understood in relation to short-term memory. Short-term memory refers to the simple maintenance of information in memory during a few seconds or minutes, whereas working memory refers to the capacity to maintain information while simultaneously processing (i.e., storing, manipulating, inhibiting, and updating) other information. Differently put, working memory is the ability to maintain multiple task-relevant representations in the face of distracting irrelevant information (combat interference). It is easy to perceive that our working memory capacity is limited. For instance, try to do this mental calculation within 10 seconds:

$23 \times 34.$

It is hard, right? Next time try this experiment on your friends or families when walking together. Ask them to do this mental calculation and see whether they can keep their walking speed. There is a high probability they will stop to calculate, because the mental calculation consumes all our working memory so there is not enough left to control walking. Similarly, mind wandering during a class or meeting prevents us from hearing what the teacher or presenter is saying. Playing smartphone games, texting, or speaking on a cell phone while driving reduces our ability to detect risks and make appropriate responses. Cell phone use while driving increases the risk of collision by over 400%, whether it is a hand-held or hand-free phone. Beginners of social dances find it difficult to hear the music because they are too busy focusing on remembering new steps. These examples show the limitation of working memory. Psychologists have devised different tasks to capture this limited working memory, and the 2-back task used by Ishihara is one such task.

In this task, subjects had to indicate whether the item (a number) was the same as or different from the item presented two trials earlier (see figure below). In the example of the following figure, the last item was the same as the item two trials earlier: both were "1."

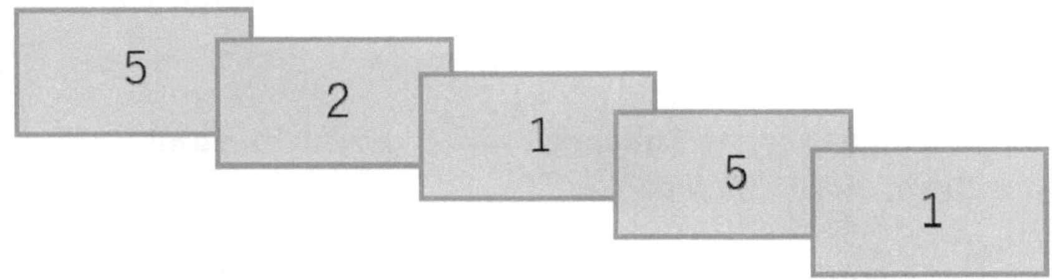

The better the subject stores and recalls the target item two trials earlier (goal-relevant information) despite having to simultaneously store the item one trial earlier (goal-irrelevant information), the higher the person's working memory capacity. Ishihara found that, in elementary school children, taking a tennis lesson for just 50 minutes improved these children's performance on this 2-back task. Compared to their baseline performance, they showed high working memory capacity after the lesson.

The Significance of Ishihara's Findings

Stressed, depressed, sleep deprived, and anxious people show lower executive function. They are poor at reasoning and solving novel problems. The lower executive function brings them more stress, negative mood, and sleep disturbance. A vicious circle. Further, with the developmental progress from childhood through early adulthood, executive function becomes increasingly efficient. Finally, during the aging process, executive function shows a gradual decline.

Ishihara's finding is exciting in that if playing tennis for only 50 minutes improves executive function, then exercise may be a powerful strategy to improve general intelligence, to promote children's cognitive development, and to solve the cognitive problems caused by stress, depression, sleep deprivation, anxiety, and aging. But the question is, does the benefit of exercise persist? Do people with high fitness levels show higher executive function than those with low fitness levels? Do people who exercise regularly show higher executive function than those who don't?

Does Regular Exercise Enhance Executive Function and Make Your Brain More Efficient?

The answer is yes. Fitness brings prolonged benefits to the brain. In a more recent study, Ishihara found that children with higher fitness had higher executive function than other children. Meanwhile, after statistically ruling out the effect of age, BMI, and fitness levels, boys with longer total years of tennis experience showed higher cognitive flexibility. This means that for boys, the more years they played tennis, the more flexibly they thought. Tennis itself is cognitively stimulating. Thus, no matter how old you are, how much your body weight is, and how bad you are at the physical test, as long as you keep playing tennis, you will acquire more cognitive flexibility over time.

Psychologists Arthur Kramer and Charles Hillman at the University of Illinois at Urbana-Champaign, who we met earlier, also investigated the effect of aerobic fitness and exercise on executive function. In a study of second- and third-year elementary school students, they found that children with high levels of fitness showed better executive function than less fit children. Then Hillman and Kramer waited for three years until these students were at the end of fourth and fifth grade and tested them again. Importantly, an increase in aerobic fitness during the three-year period was associated with a corresponding improvement in executive function. Hillman and Kramer speculated that intense exercise training, which boosts aerobic fitness, would be particularly effective in enhancing children's executive function. In a later study, they set out to test this hypothesis.

They randomly assigned 7-9 year old children to either a 9-month exercise or a control group. Only the exercise group received a 2-hour exercise session following each school day. The exercise session focused on improving fitness through engagement in many age-appropriate physical activities. These activities included moderate- to vigorous-intensity aerobic exercise, muscular strength training, and low organizational games centered on a skill theme (dribbling, throwing, catching). Additionally, the children were encouraged to continue their participation in exercise with their families on weekends.

Nine months later, children in both groups showed improvement in aerobic fitness and executive function. During this period, children experienced critical physical and cognitive development, which itself improved fitness and executive function. But the improvement in fitness and executive function was bigger in the exercise group, suggesting that exercise boosts the development of fitness and executive function.

To look at how the brain is involved, while the children were performing an executive function task, Hillman and Kramer scanned their brain using Functional Magnetic Resonance Imaging (FMRI). FMRI measures brain activity by detecting changes associated with blood flow. It relies on the observation that when the activity of a brain area increases, blood flow and blood oxygenation in that region also increase. Hillman and Kramer found that coupled with the improvements in the performance of executive function from pre- to post-training, children in the exercise group showed decreased brain activation in the right anterior prefrontal cortex. Children in the control group did not show such decrease. The reduced activation in the right anterior prefrontal cortex in the exercise group reflects greater efficiency of the brain in achieving effective performance. On similar tasks, people with higher IQ show lower (more efficient) brain activation in the prefrontal cortex. Indeed, after nine months of training, these 7-9 year old children in the exercise group showed similar performance and anterior frontal brain patterns on the task compared to a group of sedentary 22-year old adults. Striking, isn't it? Nine months of intense exercise training boosts brain efficiency equal to that of 13-15 years of natural cognitive development.

The benefit of exercise on executive function persists. Individuals who exercise regularly have higher executive function than those who don't. Individuals with high fitness show higher executive function than those with low fitness. Exercise is a powerful strategy to improve general intelligence and promote children's cognitive development. As will be discussed in later chapters, it is also a powerful strategy to solve the cognitive problems related to stress, depression, sleep deprivation, anxiety, and aging. Going back to the earlier finding that physically active children perform better at school, now we understand why that is. Physically active children have high executive function. In short, their brains are more efficient.

~~~

CHAPTER 4
People Who Exercise Regularly Have Better Memories

Those who cannot remember the past are condemned to repeat it.

— George Santayana, *Reason in Common Sense*, volume 1 of *The Life of Reason* (1905)

Regular exercise improves our capacity to memorize. In another study, using structural MRI, Hillman, Kramer, and their colleagues estimated the structural volume of different brain areas in children. They found that children with high fitness had brains with a bigger hippocampus: the seat of memories. The hippocampus is named after its resemblance to the seahorse and is critically involved in forming memories.

Our knowledge of the functions of the hippocampus is mostly inspired by the Canadian neuroscientist Brenda Milner's observation of a patient H.M. H.M. suffered from severe epileptic seizures. As a treatment, his medial temporal lobe, which includes the hippocampus, was surgically removed. After that, H.M. suffered from severe memory loss despite showing normal general intelligence. He lost the ability to form new memories and kept forgetting the names of persons whom he had just met. Despite having repeated a task several times at different occasions, he could not remember having ever completed such task. He also kept forgetting object locations. H.M. described his condition as "like waking from a dream…every day is alone in itself." It turns out that the hippocampus, the brain structure H.M. lost, plays a pivotal role in forming episodic memory (memory of episodic events), in spatial memory and navigation, and in transforming short-term memory (which lasts seconds to minutes) into long-term memory (which lasts hours to years).

Physically Active People Have Bigger Hippocampus and Better Memory

Children with higher aerobic fitness have a bigger hippocampus and therefore have better memory. Meanwhile, regular exercise increases people's capacity to remember and learn visual and verbal word lists, faces, pictures, and many other forms of information. Going back to the finding that physically active children perform better at school, we now know the second reason why this is the case. Physically active children are better at remembering what is taught by the teachers and what is written in textbooks. Exercise provides children with another powerful means to achieve success at school.

It is helpful to note that many experiences damage the hippocampus. Poverty, childhood maltreatment, aging, stress, depression, hormone therapies, hypertension, and chronic heavy drinking reduce the volume of the hippocampus and cause memory deficits. For instance, one study carried out by researchers from the British Medical Research Council and the University of Cambridge showed that along the aging process from 18 to 88, people show a decreased volume of the hippocampus and performance on memory.

This observation is true even after ruling out the influence of educational level and fluid intelligence.

In a 2011 study, Kirk Erickson at the University of Pittsburgh found that aerobic exercise reverses aging-induced hippocampal loss. The aerobic exercise consisted of 40 minutes of moderate-intensity (50-60% of maximum heart rate for the first seven weeks and 60-75% after that) walking three times a week. After participating in the aerobic exercise for a year, older adults aged 55-80 showed a 7.8% increase in the aerobic fitness level. This improvement in fitness was associated with an increase in the hippocampal volume and improvement in spatial memory. Across a one-year period, people in the walking program showed a 2% increase in the volume of the hippocampus. In contrast, in older adults of a control group who did not attend the program, the hippocampal volume decreased by 1.4%. One year of aerobic training reverses aging-related hippocampal loss by more than two years.

Thus, exercise is a potent strategy to prevent the hippocampal volume loss and memory deficits caused by poverty, childhood maltreatment, aging, stress, depression, hormone therapies, hypertension, and chronic heavy drinking.

Regular Exercise Increases Brain-Derived Neurotrophic Factor

Hillman, Kramer, and colleagues made another discovery that explains why people with high fitness have a bigger hippocampus. The increase in the hippocampal volume, they found, was associated with an increase in serum levels of brain-derived neurotrophic factor (BDNF). BDNF is a member of the neurotrophin family of growth factors (proteins). It supports the production, growth, differentiation, and survival of neurons.

Exercise and fitness increase serum levels of BDNF, which increases the number of neurons and leads to a bigger hippocampus.

Exercise Increases the Number of Neurons in the Brain

More than ten years ago before Hillman and Kramer's study, neuroscientists had reported that exercise and fitness increases the number of neurons in the brain. This holds true for children, adults, and the elderly. This observation was first made in adults, and where a story and a breakthrough in neuroscience accompanied these observations.

For the vast majority of the twentieth century, leading neuroscientists considered the nervous system incapable of regeneration. Neurons only died and could not be renewed. We are born with all our neurons, and no new neurons could be produced after birth. Yet, in the 1960s, American biologist Joseph Altman discovered that neurons continued to be generated in an adult rat's brain, particularly in the dentate gyrus of the hippocampus. This discovery was unfortunately ignored for three decades by the scientific community. However, in the early 1990s, adult neurogenesis was reconfirmed by several groups of researchers and identified in mice. In 1998, Elizabeth Gould at Princeton University reported neurogenesis in adult monkeys. In the same year, Fred Gage at the Salk Institute for Biological Studies in La Jolla, California showed that the human brain, specifically the dentate gyrus of the hippocampus, produces new neurons even into adulthood. Finally adult neurogenesis was accepted by the mainstream scientific community.

In the dentate gyrus, as much as 6% of the total number of neurons are generated each month. The newborn neurons are required for a process called behavioral pattern separation. This process transforms similar experiences into distinct and nonoverlapping memory representations. In brief, these newborn neurons make our memory more accurate.

Henriette van Praag, who worked with Fred Gage, has found that exercise promotes neurogenesis in mice. She raised mice in cages either with (runners) or without (controls) a running wheel. Four weeks later, she checked the number of newborn neurons and found that runners had 100% more newborn neurons. Running increased neurogenesis. More neurons make the memory more accurate. Accompanying the increased neurons in the mice brain, their spatial memory also improved.

The finding that exercise increases the creation of new neurons is exciting. But can exercise increase the number of new neurons in the human brain? To answer this question, Fred Gage's team identified a marker for neurogenesis in humans. They found that the proliferative clusters in the dentate gyrus were associated with growing capillaries in the same region. Most of the dividing cells were at the growing terminus of small capillaries. It suggests that neurogenesis occurs within an angiogenic niche. More neurogenesis is associated with more capillaries. The increase in capillaries induces increased cerebral blood volume (CBV). CBV can be directly detected in humans by perfusion techniques. Gage's team confirmed that wheel running increased the CBV in the dentate gyrus of mice, which was correlated with postmortem measurements of neurogenesis. They then employed the dentate gyrus CBV as a marker of neurogenesis to study the effect of exercise on the human brain.

Pereira asked subjects aged 21-45 years old to exercise for 12 weeks. The subjects did one hour of cycling, treadmill running, climbing, and so on four times a week. Pereira found that the 12 weeks of exercise increased dentate gyrus CBV, which was correlated with a subject's performance in a later short-term memory test. This provided the first evidence that exercise promoted neurogenesis in humans. More neurons endow physically active individuals with an enhanced capacity to memorize various information in daily life.

~~~

CHAPTER 5
Brisk Walking for Ten Minutes Is Sufficient to Boost Positive Mood

Self-actualizing people, that is, psychologically healthy, psychologically "superior" people are better cognizers and perceivers. This may be true even at the sensory level itself; for example, it would not surprise me if they turned out to be more acute about differentiating fine hue differences, etc.

— Abraham Maslow, *The Farther Reaches Of Human Nature* (1993)

In November 2016, I went to San Diego, California to attend the annual scientific meeting of the Society for Neuroscience. One day after the meeting, my colleagues and I went to La Jolla Beach to see the sunset. The beach is just five miles south to the Salk Institute for Biological Studies in La Jolla, where Fred Gage discovered adult human neurogenesis. East to the Pacific Ocean, the La Jolla Beach provides a perfect view of the ocean and an amazing sea of color as the sun goes down. As we were enjoying the sea and sunset, a young-looking elderly lady walked by and stopped to chat with us about the beautiful scene. Several minutes later, her husband, a tall, aged but vigorous man, with his upper body naked and a dog with him, came to us. It turned out that he was the 2001 Nobel Prize winner in Chemistry K. Barry Sharpless! He and his wife were walking on the beach with their dog. In fact, they had been doing so for more than 20 years. They said walking in the beautiful scene made them healthy, happy and helped them enjoy life more.

This encounter reminded me of a study performed by my friend, Lili Yue at Hokkaido University. When I was attending Professor Masao Mizuno's Physical Fitness seminar, Lili Yue, then a master student in Professor Yoshinori Ohtsuka's lab, was doing a project on forest bathing (saunter in the woods). Professor Ohtsuka is an expert on hot spring and natural medicine. Lili was investigating the therapeutic effect of forest bathing. She found several walking trails perfect for forest bathing on our campus. Our campus was covered with woods, rivers, ponds, and farms. It was especially beautiful in the summer when Lili did her research. Lili asked college students to walk along the trails she specified. She then did a lot of physiological and questionnaire measurements before and after the walks. One interesting result she found out was, the students were more energetic and felt more refreshed after 30 minutes of walking along the trails.

Two fundamental factors here may have contributed to the enhanced positive mood in Lili's subjects and in Sharpless and his wife: the natural environment (forest and ocean) and exercise. Whereas Lili and Professor Ohtsuka focused more on the benefit of the natural environment, I was attracted to the idea that exercise boosts positive mood and promotes mental health.

Even Brief Exercise Increases Positive Mood

Three decades ago, at California State University, 100 miles northwest to the La Jolla Beach where we came across Sharpless and his wife, psychologist Robert Thayer made a pioneering discovery. Brisk walking for just ten minutes is sufficient to increase people's energy and optimism. It is also enough to decrease their tension and perceived seriousness of personal problems. Some effects may last for as long as two hours after only ten minutes of walking. So next time your friends or family become pessimistic or upset when talking about any particular problem, ask them to go out for a walk with you. Ten minutes later, you will find them more optimistic and less upset. Walking makes it easier to talk to them about problems.

When stressed, many people eat sugary snacks (which is called comfort food) or smoke to relieve the intense feeling. These two coping strategies do, in the short term, reduce the negative feeling. But in the long run, they are detrimental to both physical and mental health (e.g., see Chapter 12). Thayer found that brisk walking for ten minutes was more effective in improving the feeling of being energetic and lowering tension than eating a candy bar. Also, a 5-minute walk before smoking a cigarette or eating a sugary snack considerably reduced the urge to smoke or snack. The 5-minute walk also lengthened the time until the next cigarette was smoked or snack was eaten. It then suggests that exercise can be a substitute for smoking or snacking to boost positive mood and reduce stress. Not only walking, but other physical activities are also effective. In yet another study, 15 minutes of running, playing volleyball, space hoppers, or skipping ropes substantially boosted positive mood in children. Thus, after 15 minutes of exercise, these kids were more cheerful, happy, pleased, friendly, active, energetic, and excited.

Depending on what kind of exercise you do, the mood-enhancing effect of an acute episode of exercise generally reaches its peak in about half an hour. After that, the enhanced positive mood gradually returns to basal level. So, does regular exercise improve the basal mood? Are individuals who exercise regularly happier and more positive than those who don't? Yes. A meta-analysis of 70 studies published between 1945 and 2004 has reported that exercising for as short as 4-6 weeks is effective in enhancing basal mood. The effect size was estimated to be 0.37. This effect size was comparable to that of regular exercise on reading skills (0.36) we mentioned in Chapter 2. People in daily life should have readily perceived an effect size of this magnitude. In one study, scientists asked people to list the most effective strategies they used to regulate mood in their daily life. Most people listed exercise as the number one effective strategy. Here are the rankings scientists summarized based on people's answers.

(1) Exercise

(2) Listening to music

(3) Calling, talking to or being with someone

(4) Tending to chores

(5) Resting, napping or sleeping

(6) Using cognitive regulation strategies such as control thoughts, checking or analyzing the situation, and putting feelings in perspective

(7) Avoiding the thing/person causing the mood

(8) Being alone

Furthermore, another recent research using a multiplatform smartphone application asked over 28,000 people to report their real-time mood and mood regulation strategies over four weeks. It was found that when people felt bad, they participated in sports most often, followed by approaching nature, engaging in leisure activities, chatting, participating in cultural activities, drinking, playing, eating, and so on. More importantly, doing sports produced the greatest mood-enhancing effect compared to all other activities. The ranking of the effectiveness of the strategies people used is shown here,

(1) Sports

(2) Nature

(3) Culture

(4) Leisure

(5) Chatting

(6) Drinking

(7) Playing

(8) Eating

We have listed substantial evidence on how exercise boosts positive mood. Yet, a more fundamental question is: why do we need positive moods? Certainly, the experience of positive moods feels great. But is that all? No. Positive moods bring more than a great feeling.

Positive Moods Broaden Attention

We have this everyday experience: when we feel happy and high, our vision broadens, and we can notice many things all at once. When we feel sad and bad, our vision narrows, and we easily focus on particular parts of things. That is because positive moods broaden while negative moods narrow the scope of our attention. Attention is the lower part of cognition. It delivers information to working memory for higher processing. A positive mood and a broader scope of attention allows us to take in more information.

In an insightful neuroimaging study, psychologists showed subjects a series of compound images that featured human faces in a central location surrounded by images of houses. Participants were asked to indicate whether the face in each compound image was male or female. They didn't have to look at the surrounding houses. It has been well established that one particular brain area, the extrastriate fusiform area (EFA), activates when we look at human faces. A distinct brain area, the parahippocampal place area (PPA), activates when we look at places. In this study, all the subjects, whether in positive, neutral, or negative mood, showed similar activation of the EFA. It therefore suggests that people in different moods respond similarly to the centrally put faces. However, relative to neutral mood, subjects with positive moods showed greater activation in the PPA. These subjects were paying more attention to the background house. With positive moods, people take in more of the contextual surroundings. Positive moods give individual a broader field of view in visual neural encoding. In contrast, people with negative moods displayed a decreased activation in the PPA. That is, negative moods narrowed their field of view.

Positive Mood Increases Creative Thoughts

Along with the broadened attention, positive mood also expands our creative and flexible thoughts. In the laboratory, psychologists has noticed that individuals with positive moods show higher creativity when completing various cognitive tasks.

For instance, individuals with positive moods are better at the often used Candle Task.

In this task, subjects are presented with a box of tacks, a candle, and a book of matches. They are asked to attach the candle to the wall (a corkboard) so it will burn without dripping wax on the table or floor. The difficulty of this problem arises from the functional fixedness of the box. The box is a container of thumb-tacks in the problem. But it must be a shelf in the solution. Conventional thinking prevents people from breaking the functional fixedness of the box. Psychologists have found that subjects with a positive mood consistently outperform those with a neutral or negative mood in this task. With positive mood, subjects can easily go beyond the conventional functional fixedness of the tacks box and creatively use it as a shelf.

People with positive mood also perform better on the Local-Global Task, the one employed by Ishihara to evaluate cognitive flexibility. Individuals with positive moods can flexibly switch between thinking in different levels and dimensions. Compared to neutral or negative mood, positive mood more readily activates our accumulated knowledge because of a more broadened attention inwards. This allows us to flexibly manipulate our overall knowledge, consciously or unconsciously, and be more creative.

Happy Students Learn More at School

Positive mood broadens our attention and boosts our creativity and cognitive flexibility. Given the significance of attention, creativity and cognitive flexibility for learning, positive mood thus promotes successful academic performance. Students with more positive moods are better at learning. In a 1991 experiment, Tanis Bryan at the University of Illinois asked half of the students to close their eyes and count silently from 1 to 50, while he asked the other half of the students to close their eyes and think of a happy moment in their lives. This simple manipulation induced neutral versus happy mood in these students. Bryan found that compared to those in the neutral mood, students in the happy mood solved more math problems. Recently Sara Scrimin at the University of Padova, Italia replicated this finding in college students. Scrimin asked college students to read a scientific text. Compared to those who had viewed a tragedy video clip, those who had seen a comedy clip comprehended the text better and gleaned more factual knowledge from the text.

Given the benefits of a positive mood, I hope now you can fully appreciate the role exercise plays in enhancing mood.

~~

CHAPTER 6
Physically Active Individuals Experience Less Stress

A healthy mind in a healthy body.

— Roman poet Juvenal

Imagine being a volunteer for an experiment. You are in the laboratory of a psychology department and are asked to immerse your left hand into a basin of icy water for 60 seconds. "It is cold!" You say after immersing your hand into the water. You do not know the exact temperature of the water, but you can feel pain in your hand. You want to get your hand out of the icy water as soon as possible. But you recall that the experiment only lasts for 60 seconds, and it is no more than a single painful experience; you hang on until the end.

Imagine you are attending another experiment. You are asked to give a 5-minute speech introducing yourself. In front of you are two well-dressed and serious interviewers. Naturally, you are puzzled, wondering what you should say about yourself. While you are giving the speech, you occasionally hear one interviewer say: "You are slow," "Come on, hurry up." You get nervous. Anyhow, you finish the speech and are then asked to perform a 5-minute mental arithmetic before those same interviewers. Your task is to subtract seven from any number they give you serially before it gets to the negatives. But it seems no matter how fast you calculate, the "unfriendly" interviewer always tells you to "go faster." It is tough.

These two procedures are common stressors employed by psychologists in the laboratory. The first one is a physical stressor, while the second one is a social stressor. Both induce significant physiological and psychological responses. When exposed to either of them, physiologically, people show increases in heart rate, blood pressure, levels of body arousal and the stress hormone cortisol. Psychologically, people report increases in stress, anxiety, depression, and even anger.

Interestingly, when subjected to these two stressors, individuals who perform better on the shuttle run test, that is, individuals with high fitness show less physiological and psychological responses. They show less increases in heart rate, blood pressure, and the levels of arousal and cortisol. They report less increases in the feelings of stress, anxiety, depression, and anger. Similarly, people who exercise regularly, even just once per week, show less physiological and psychological responses compared to those who don't.

To buffer stress response, exercise does not have to be too long. In a recent study using the above cold water stressor, children who just played physically active games (e.g., run and catch, dodgeball and capture the flag) for 30 minutes demonstrated decreased physiological stress responses. In contrast, children who watched TV or played physically inactive video games for 30 minutes did not show such decrease. In another study carried out in adults, 25 minutes of cycling buffered the subsequent stress response in a paradigm similar to the above public speech social stressor. These findings suggest that exercise relieves our experience of stress. In this chapter, we will look at the detrimental effects of chronic stress and see how exercise protects us from overexposure to stress in everyday life.

A Double-Edged Sword: The Stress Response

Faced with (an anticipated) threat, to improve the chance of survival, our body activates a broad range of responses including the nervous, endocrine, and immune systems. These responses are collectively known as the stress response. The fastest response is initiated by the autonomic nervous system (ANS). Within seconds, ANS increases our heart rate, blood pressure, and arousal levels. All prepare us for a fight-or-flight response. However, excitation of ANS is short-term and wanes fast. Activation of the hypothalamic-pituitary-adrenocortical (HPA) axis, which leads to the release of the stress hormone cortisol, induces long-lasting effects. Cortisol mobilizes the stored energy of our body and potentiates the sympathetically mediated ANS effects to cope with danger, such as arousal. Depending on the stressors, cortisol peaks after tens of minutes and then gradually decreases to a normal level after one or two hours.

Cortisol functions through activating its receptors. In the last half a century, a broad distribution of cortisol receptors was found in our brain. The distribution is particularly rich in regions responsible for executive function, memory, and emotion regulation, such as the prefrontal cortex (PFC) and hippocampus. This rich expression of cortisol provides a structural basis for cortisol to mobilize the brain to cope with stressors that require higher cognitive processing in the PFC and hippocampus. For instance, in the above cold water situation, the PFC and hippocampus assure you that it is only a painful experience and lasts just 60s. In the public speech case, the PFC and hippocampus are responsible for thinking of what ways you can present yourself and effectively cope with the situation. Finally, during both these situations the PFC and hippocampus evaluate the situation. Once they think you are safe, they provide negative feedback signals to the HPA axis, which eventually shuts off the stress response and brings the increased cortisol level down to normal.

The stress response is evolutionarily adaptive. It is necessary for active coping with the environment and survival. However, if the response is frequent or prolonged, in the case of repeated or chronic stress, it will induce maladaptive changes, and damage the body and brain. Perhaps you have heard people say anger is bad for your body and heart. Anger is a typical stress response. Frequent anger causes repeated increases in heart rate and blood pressure, which poses a significant threat to the cardiovascular system and increases the risk of hypertension, heart attack and stroke. In addition, repeated anger, like other chronic stress, is detrimental to the brain and mind.

Chronic Stress Damages the Brain

People experience many forms of chronic stress in daily life. Chronic pain, obesity (it causes a robust stress response in the body and brain, see Chapter 12), childhood trauma (such as maltreatment), poverty, prolonged unemployment, financial hardship, marital conflict, work overload, and shiftwork, are typical examples of chronic stress. They can cause a hyperactivity of the HPA axis and leads to a continuously high level of cortisol.

High levels of cortisol, through its rich receptors, induce a continuous, over activation of neurons in the PFC and hippocampus.

The continuous and over activation of neurons eventually causes pathological processes that damage and kill those neurons. Besides, high levels of cortisol also reduce the amount of neurotrophic factors such as BDNF. BDNF is necessary for the growth and survival of neurons. It therefore also inhibits the generation of new neurons in the hippocampus. The result is a damaged, structurally smaller and functionally weaker PFC and hippocampus. As we have said, the PFC and hippocampus are the structural basis for executive function and memory, which are essential for problem-solving and learning. Further, the PFC and hippocampus provide negative feedback control of the HPA axis and bring down the cortisol levels to normal. Thus, individuals with damaged PFC and hippocampus will encounter more stress and have an even higher level of cortisol hence poor executive function and memory: a vicious circle.

For example, according to a recent German study carried out by Martin Driessen at Gilead Hospital, Bielefeld, adults with a history of childhood trauma have a smaller hippocampal volume. Specifically, as high as a 24% interpersonal difference in hippocampal volume in adulthood could be attributed to childhood trauma.

Accompanying the high levels of cortisol and reduced brain volume of the PFC and hippocampus, people with high levels of chronic stress show severe cognitive deficits. They have lower executive function and memory. As a result, they perform poorly at school and work.

Stressed Students Have Lower Cognitive Ability and Perform Poorly at School

Compared to their less-stressed peers, students with high levels of stress perform poorly on almost every major subjects, including English, math, science, and technology. Stress not only attenuates their ability to learn and remember during classes, but also reduces their ability to recall what they have learned and remembered in the past during exams.

Students may suffer from stress at home. Poverty, maltreatment, and exposure to domestic violence reduce children's cognitive abilities and academic achievement significantly. Several well-designed studies have estimated that children raised in households that fall below the poverty threshold have IQs that are on average 12-18 points lower than their peers raised in upper-middle-class families, such as households of doctors or lawyers. The lower IQ predisposes them to score up to 10% lower on standardized tests at school. Furthermore, poverty is associated with more hostile parenting behaviors, more home chaos (e.g., homes that are less structured, more crowded, noisy), less parental support (see Chapter 10), and more stressful life events such as the frequent changing of schools. All these have been associated with poor cognitive ability and low academic achievement. Moreover, children exposed to maltreatment (such as corporal punishment) or domestic violence have been reported to possess lower IQs of about 3-9 points than those that are not. Notably, in a U.S. national survey of 2-9 years old children, each increase of one extra spanking per week reported by the mother was associated with a roughly 1.1 points decrease in IQ four years later.

Students may also be stressed from their peers and teachers at school. Bullying at school by peers and the spillover of stress from teachers to students have been attracting lots of research attention. Several large-scale reports have shown that victims of school bullying have lower grades at school. Students in schools with higher levels of bullying on average have lower grade point average (GPA). Furthermore, students from classes of stressed teachers perceive more stress and report less support from their teachers.

Because of this spillover of stress, students' academic achievement is negatively associated with teachers' stress level. For instance, a German study found that the more emotionally exhausted the elementary school teachers were, the lower math scores their students had. This finding was true even after statistically ruling out the influence of the teachers' years of experience, teaching certifications, and the students' socioeconomic status and cognitive ability. In this study, the adverse influence of the teachers' emotional exhaustion well exceeded the positive impact of teachers' years of experience. That is, students from classes of new (i.e., with little teaching experience) but happy teachers outperformed students from classes of experienced but stressed teachers. Two reasons underlie this observation. First, the teachers' stress may have spilled over to their students. Stressed students perform poorly. Second, the stressed teachers themselves may have been suffering from reduced teaching ability. They could not effectively use their knowledge and teaching skills that they had gained through their education and experience.

Physically Active Individuals Experience Less Stress

Chronic stress is toxic. Thus, finding effective strategies to cope with chronic stress in daily life has been a fundamental inquiry in modern science. In this context, the finding that physically active people show reduced stress responses is of crucial importance. In the laboratory, individuals with high levels of fitness and people who exercise regularly (even just once per week) have reduced physiological and psychological response to stress. Further, playing physically active games or cycling for just 25-30 minutes is enough to buffer later stress response.

In line with the findings in the laboratory, exercise has been proven effective in buffering real life stress. As we've mentioned earlier, in the 1980s, Robert Thayer at California State University reported that only ten minutes of brisk walking was enough to reduce the perceived seriousness of personal problems. In another 2012 study, Birinder Cheema at University of Western Sydney, Australia reported that 15 minutes of yoga reduced stress at the workplace. During work time, Cheema asked office employees to perform either their usual work or yoga postures while seated in a chair for 15 minutes. The employees who performed yoga postures reported reduced stress and showed reduced physiological markers of stress.

Meanwhile, population-based surveys of vocational students, medical residents, teachers, healthcare or governmental workers have shown those engaging in high levels of exercise (be it aerobic or resistance), especially vigorous exercise, have low levels of stress, fatigue, and depression in their daily life. Further, increases in exercise, such as swimming, yoga, running, jogging, or dance, is associated with a corresponding decrease in perceived stress, fatigue, anxiety, depression, and an increase in energy and vigor.

Given the robust evidence that exercise reduces people's experience of stress and that exercise promotes academic achievement, recently, exercise has been suggested as one potential strategy to reduce the achievement gap between students from low and high socioeconomic status. Exercise as one such strategy is promising for it is cheap and easily available.

Finally, I'm compelled to highlight a personal experience that is "nice-to-know." After reading the draft of this chapter, a friend commented: "If we ask the maltreated and bullied students to exercise, they will feel less stress and show improvement in academic achievement." This statement is true. However, it is worth noting that exercise is not enough and not the optimal solution to the problem of repeated maltreatment and bullying. We should attempt to solve the problem of maltreatment and bullying first. In this regard, the insight of Plato (i.e., *In order for man to succeed in life, God provided him with two means, education and physical activity. Not separately, one for the soul and the other for the body, but for the two together. With these two means, man can attain perfection.*) is helpful. Educate the perpetrators of maltreatment and bullying and ask them to exercise, as exercise improves self-control and reduces anger and impulsivity (see next chapter).

~~~

CHAPTER 7
Students Who Regularly Exercise Are Better at Self-discipline

We know what it is to get out of bed on a freezing morning in a room without a fire, and how the very vital principle within us protests against the idea. Probably most persons have lain on certain mornings for an hour at a time unable to brace themselves to the resolve. We think how late we shall be, how the duties of the day will suffer; we say, "I must get up, this is ignominious," and so on. But still the warm couch feels too delicious, and the cold outside too cruel, and resolution faints away and postpones itself again and again just as it seemed on the verge of the decisive act.

— William James, *The Principles of Psychology* (1890)

In the 1970s, psychologist Daryl Bem at Stanford University attempted to study conscientiousness as a psychological trait. He tried to distinguish conscientious people, who were supposed to be organized and efficient, from others by sorting out a list of behaviors. He inferred that students who turn in school assignments on time also tended to wear clean socks every day, since both would stem from the same trait of conscientiousness. But when he gathered data from Stanford students, he found quite the opposite. The students who turned in their homework on time were less likely to wear clean socks every day. The students who wore clean socks every day were less likely to turn in their homework on time.

More than three decades later, two Australian psychologists, Megan Oaten and Ken Cheng at Macquarie University, noticed something similar. As it came closer to the end of a semester, when the students had to take exams and turn in assignments, they tended to keep more smelly socks and clothes in their dormitory. The students could either study hard for the finals or wash their socks and clothes, but not both. Also during finals, they ate more junk food, exercised less, failed to wash dishes and their hair, and did not shave. They were also more likely to miss appointments and commitments. This was clearly not to save time, because they also overslept, smoked more and consumed more caffeine. Although there were fewer parties, they drank as much as ever. Further, they were more easily offended and impulsive in spending. In summary, the healthy lifestyle and conscientiousness of the students all disappeared. Oaten and Cheng reasoned that during finals, these students must have been suffering from "ego depletion." Ego depletion is a phenomenon due to the failure of self-regulation proposed by social psychologist Roy Baumeister at Florida State University.

According to Baumeister, behaviors that need effortful self-regulation, such as decision-making, stress coping, emotion regulation, resisting desires, temptations, or impulses, all share the same cognitive resource. More importantly, this shared cognitive resource is limited and easily depleted. The previous self-regulation may cause the depletion of the resource which reduces the ability of subsequent self-regulation. This depleted state is called "ego depletion" by Baumeister. When depleted, people lose their "willpower" and fail to regulate their behaviors, emotions, and thoughts.

This is exactly what happened to the college students above. The academic examinations and assignments posed a great stress to them, which depleted their self-regulation resource and induced ego depletion. During the exam period, these students failed to maintain their healthy lifestyle and conscientiousness. Neither could they control their emotions, that's why they were more easily offended. In this chapter, we will look at this ego depletion phenomenon and its influences. After that, we will see how regular exercise effectively improves one's self-regulation capacity.

The Failure of Self-Regulation

Baumeister had been long interested in studying people's desires and attempts to control desires in everyday life. He once asked over 200 adults to wear beepers from morning till evening each day for a week. During this period, at which people typically stay awake, Baumeister randomly selected a signal time and asked subjects, through the beepers, to report their active desire(s). Later, Baumeister collected the data and analyzed people's desires across the whole week. He found that, on half of the occasions at which people were beeped, they indicated at least one active desire. The most common desires were to eat, sleep, drink, media use, leisure, social contact, hygiene-related activities, smoking, sex, work, coffee, alcohol, engagement in sports, and spending. People reported that, among all the desires, 47% conflicted with their other motivations or goals. Most conflicting desires (42%) was resisted, while the rest (5%) was enacted.

Regarding people's attempt to control their desires, an interesting phenomenon occurred. The more frequent previously people tried to resist a desire, the less likely they successfully resisted a later desire on the same day.

Why does previously attempts to resist a desire impair people's ability to resist a later desire? Psychologists call the process of overriding one's thoughts, behaviors, and emotions, and replacing them with those more in line with one's primary goals self-regulation or self-control. Does it suggest that people's capacity of self-regulation is limited? Does the previous usage of self-regulation diminish people's available self-regulation resource for later use? To answer these questions, Baumeister developed an experimental paradigm. He asked subjects to perform two tasks in a row. The first task was used to consume or deplete their capacity of self-regulation. Examples were resisting the temptation of delicious food, giving a hard public speech, suppressing responses to emotional video clips, and performing a complex secretarial task. After the first task, the second task was used to measure and quantify people's performance on self-regulation. Examples were solving puzzles, executive function tasks, and emotion regulation tasks. If people's capacity of self-regulation is limited, then compared to those who only take the second task, people who have finished the first task, having their self-regulation resources depleted, will perform poorly on the second task. This indeed was what Baumeister observed. In a series of experiments, those who had taken the first task gave up earlier in the second puzzle-solving task, responded much slower and with lesser accuracy in the second executive function task. After the second task, they also felt more passive.

Baumeister proposed that people's capacity to perform self-regulation over a period of time is limited and easily depleted. Their previous self-regulation may cause a depletion, which reduces the ability of later self-regulation. Self-regulation can be viewed as analogous to a muscle. Just as a muscle needs strength and energy to exert force over a period, acts that consume self-regulation also need strength and energy to perform. Similarly, as a muscle becomes fatigued after a period of sustained exertion and has reduced capacity to exert further force, so self-regulation also becomes depleted after the previous usage. Baumeister called this state of diminished self-regulation "ego depletion."

Many experiences that require self-regulation induce ego depletion. Based on the contents of what to regulate, these experiences can be divided into three categories:

(1) Regulating behavior, such as eating a healthy diet, cutting out smoking, drinking, and excessive financial expenditure, and self-image management

(2) Regulating emotion, such as being offended, being forgiving and tolerant towards partners' misbehavior, hiding anger before boss, controlling sexual impulses, and avoiding exposure to other stressful life events

(3) Regulating cognition, such as logical reasoning, suppressing negative thoughts and stereotypes, and other activities that use executive function

When depleted, people feel less able to exert control, fail to resist temptation and conflict, perceive tasks as more difficult than they are, report more negative affections and subjective fatigue, lower self-efficacy, easily give up (lose their "willpower"), and show more intensive and sensitive emotional reactions. At these occasions, people feel time passes slower and the minutes drag like hours.

Now let's get back to the smelly socks in the college students' dormitory. During finals, these students suffered from ego depletion. Oaten and Cheng administered the experimental paradigm developed by Baumeister to these students at different times throughout the semester. They used a thought suppression task followed by the Stroop Test. In the thought suppression task, students were asked to avoid thinking about a white bear and to mark their recording sheet whenever they did. Try it. It is a hard task. This thought suppression task consumed self-regulation and was used to induce a state of ego depletion. Following this task, the students performed the Stroop Test, which measures inhibitory control as we have introduced earlier. The Stroop Test was used to evaluate the capacity for self-regulation. Compared to the beginning and middle of the semester, students performed worse in this experimental paradigm near the end of the semester. Apparently, the pressure of exams and assignments depleted their limited self-regulation capacity. In a depleted state, the students could not maintain their healthy lifestyle and conscientiousness as usual.

Depleted Students Perform Poorly on Academic Tasks

Studying and taking exams are highly complex cognitive activities that both require self-regulation. Thus, students who suffer from ego depletion will perform poorly on academic tasks compared to those who don't. In later experiments, Baumeister asked half of the undergraduates to watch a 6-minute videotape during which they have to try "not to read or look at any words that appear on the screen." He asked the other half of the undergraduates to watch the same videotape but without giving such instruction. For the first half of the students, the task involved self-regulation of attention insofar as the students were explicitly required to manage their attention and redirect it back to the video whenever they noticed the irrelevant words. The task-induced a depleted state in the first half of the students. Following the videotape, Baumeister asked all the students to try solving complex problems from the Verbal and Analytic sections of the Graduate Record Exam (GRE). The first half of students who were depleted performed worse than the other half of students who were not depleted. The problems from the GRE involved reading and comprehending a passage and then demonstrating an interpretive understanding of the complex information. These problems have been shown to require executive function. However, when in a depleted state, students could barely solve the complex problems.

This result explains the finding that stressed students perform poorly on almost every major subject. Stress depletes the cognitive resource for self-regulation. In a depleted state, how could they effectively and efficiently solve complex problems on the exams?

When Self-Regulation Outperforms IQ

Although everyone may, sometimes, suffer from ego depletion, there does exist interpersonal differences. Some people are better at self-regulation and less likely to suffer from ego depletion than others. This individual difference turns out to be crucial to academic achievement.

The "marshmallow experiment" carried out by psychologist Walter Mischel in the 1960s is a classic in the study of individual differences in self-regulation. Marshmallows are tasty, and children love them. Mischel knew this well so he presented 4-year old preschoolers with a plate of marshmallows. He then told each child he would leave the room for a few minutes and the child had to make a simple choice. If the child waited until he returned, the child could have two marshmallows. If the child simply could not wait, the child could ring a bell, and he would come back immediately, but the child would only be allowed one marshmallow. This choice, one for now or two for later, was simple. But it brought a conflict. The child knew well that two marshmallows were better, but to wait for two future marshmallows, he/she must resist the immediate temptation of one marshmallow. It turned out that the ability to sacrifice the immediate pleasure of one chewy marshmallow to indulge in two marshmallows later, namely the ability to delay gratification, was an excellent measure of self-regulation capacity. The time the children could wait before taking the marshmallows was associated with several psychological and educational outcomes.

Mischel followed up with these children for more than a decade until they were in high school. The children who at four years old waited longer before taking the marshmallow were better able to concentrate, plan, tolerate frustration, and cope with stress. They also had higher scores on the Scholastic Aptitude Test (SAT). This interpersonal difference in the delay time before taking the marshmallow explained 17.3% and 32.5% of the interpersonal difference in the verbal and math score of SAT respectively. The capacity to delay gratification is one critical component of self-regulation, which is crucial for regulating studying related behaviors. Mischel speculated those children who were better able to resist temptation were better able to regulate their thoughts, emotions, and behaviors and thus better able to hit the books, concentrate and devote more time to learning when they got older.

More than four decades after Mischel's study, positive psychologists Angela Duckworth and Martin Seligman made a further observation that self-regulation, or self-discipline in their wording, outperformed IQ in predicting students' academic achievement. Duckworth and Seligman measured the self-discipline of eighth-grade students in various ways. They asked the students about the degree to which they said and did things impulsively, and to which they would prefer a small, immediate reward versus a large, delayed reward. They asked parents and teachers about each student's ability to inhibit behaviors, follow the rules, and control impulsive reactions. They combined scores on all these measures into a single measure of self-discipline and then compared how well this measure predicted academic achievement half a year later and how well a standard IQ test did.

Strikingly, self-discipline was more than four-fold as important as IQ. IQ explained 10.2% of the interpersonal difference in GPA, while self-discipline explained 44.9%. IQ explained 6.8 % of the interpersonal difference in selection to high school, while self-discipline explained 31.4%. Furthermore, whereas students with higher self-discipline had higher school attendance, more hours spent doing homework, and fewer hours spent watching television, students with higher IQ showed none of these learning behaviors. Duckworth and Seligman concluded that one primary reason for students with low academic achievement is their failure to exercise self-discipline rather than their IQ. Self-discipline partly determines even IQ itself. Crystallized intelligence results from the long-term accumulation of knowledge. Fluid intelligence improves with practice. It is important to emphasize and enhance self-discipline in cognitive development and academic achievement.

Self-Regulation and Development as a Whole Person

During finals, the depleted college students dropped all their healthy lifestyles and conscientiousness. They ate more junk food, exercised less, failed to wash dishes, smelly socks, and clothes, did not wash hair and shave, and were more likely to miss appointments and commitments. They overslept, smoked more and consumed more caffeine, and were more easily offended. Furthermore, although there were fewer parties, they drank as much as ever. These behaviors characterizing the depleted students also characterize individuals with low self-regulation capacity. For instance,

(1) People with lower self-regulation eat less healthily, are worse at controlling their consumption of food, more likely to show emotional eating in response to stress, and at more risk of obesity.

(2) When insulted, individuals low in self-regulation are more likely to express intentions of behaving aggressively.

(3) People with low self-regulation are at greater risk for substance abuse and unprotected sex, more likely to suffer from alcohol-related problems, smoke, and be involved in violence and criminality.

(4) Due to their failures in regulating emotional responses, individuals with lower self-regulation show lower self-efficacy and self-esteem, more symptoms of depression, anxiety, anger, and family conflict.

Strategies to Boost Self-Regulation: Exercise Works

The neurobiological explanation of the phenomenon of ego depletion is still unclear. One popular hypothesis is that the limited cognitive resource for self-regulation depends on blood glucose levels. Depleted individuals show lower levels of blood glucose than their average levels and levels of not-depleted people. This explains why people often find themselves easily acting out of temper when feeling hungry. Also, when depleted, glucose supplementation, for instance sugared beverages, restores the performance on self-regulation tasks in depleted people. Thus, a food break or glucose supplementation with sugared beverages is an effective strategy to reboot short-term self-regulation capacity. But note that too much glucose causes obesity, another even more serious problem (see Chapter 12). Meanwhile, activities boosting positive moods, such as watching a comedy video, receiving a surprise gift, and being supported by one's partner or family members, all enhance self-regulation capacity.

We have mentioned that self-regulation is like a muscle, which may get fatigued after a period of sustained exertion. It is also true that like a muscle, self-regulation can be enhanced with practice. Training self-regulation in one domain can improve self-regulation performance in another domain. In a series of experiments by Baumeister and his collaborators, individuals who practiced self-regulation for just two weeks by monitoring and improving posture, regulating mood, monitoring and recording eating, cutting back on sweets, or squeezing a handgrip (as long as possible twice a day) showed improvement in self-regulation tasks. Wait a minute, squeezing a handgrip? Isn't that a resistance exercise?

Exercise promotes self-regulation. Regular exercise improves executive function, promotes positive mood, buffers chronic stress, which is associated with reduced ego depletion. In a recent study, Megan Oaten and Ken Cheng asked college students to engage in two months of regular exercise. The exercise consisted of 3-4 times per week of aerobic classes and resistance training. Two months later, these students showed increased self-regulation capacity. Furthermore, the smelly socks in their dormitories disappeared! The students reported decreased stress and improved emotional control. They smoked less, ate less junk food, consumed less alcohol and caffeine, were more likely to attend to their commitments and appointments, and became better at monitoring their spending. They also showed improvement in study habits. These results suggest that regular exercise enhances the capacity of self-regulation and provides support for another important means by which exercise contributes to academic achievement.

CHONG CHEN

~~~

CHAPTER 8
Exercise as Medicine: As Little as 10-29 Minutes of Daily Exercise Prevents Depression

If exercise could be packed into a pill, it would be the single most widely prescribed-and beneficial-medicine in the nation.

— Dr. Robert Butler, former director of the U.S. National Institute on Aging

In July 2016, the smartphone game app Pokémon Go was released. It soon turned into a great success. Within the first month, it had been downloaded 130 million times, which breaks a Guinness World Record. To earn points in this game, people must walk around in the real world to catch Pokémon characters, which are placed in proximity to them and shown on their smartphone screen. Interestingly, only one week following the release of the game, psychologist John Grohol, the founder & CEO of the mental health social network *Psych Central*, reported that players were using social media to share how the game helped them relieve their depression. Although whether Pokémon Go can relieve people's depression is still subject to scientific investigation, there might be at least two features of the game that contribute to an antidepressant-like effect. First, the game is rewarding. Successfully capturing a character in this game is rewarding and rewards reduce negative mood. Second, the game encourages people to physically walk around and walking reduces negative mood. This chapter will discuss the therapeutic effect of exercise for people with depression.

Depression as Learned Helplessness

In the 1960s, two graduate students at the University of Pennsylvania, Martin Seligman and Steven Maier made an unexpected observation. They found that dogs that underwent repeated stress had the tendency to develop a state of "learned helplessness." In their experiment, restrained dogs got 64 electric shocks on the first day, during which there was no way for the dogs to escape even if they tried hard. On the second day, the dogs were put into a new shuttle box, but this time they could easily escape if they jumped a short barrier between the two chambers. However, the dogs often failed to escape altogether instead they passively waited for the shock. The animals could have escaped, but they just failed to try: they had become desperate. Seligman and Maier termed this state "learned helplessness." It turns out this theory of learned helplessness explains a considerable proportion of patients with depression. Depressed people have "learned" to be helpless and desperate due to their "failure" in previous life experiences.

In humans, two major factors drive the development of learned helplessness and depression: chronic stress and psychological vulnerability. As we have seen earlier, chronic life stress, such as chronic pain, obesity, childhood maltreatment, poverty, prolonged unemployment, financial hardship, marital conflict, work overload and shiftwork damages the brain. They impair executive function and memory and reduce the capacity for self-regulation. The outcome is a dysfunctional problem-solving ability, which as a result produces more stress. This vicious circle is more emphasized in individuals with psychological vulnerabilities such as:

(1) Negative inferential style: the tendency to view negative events as caused by oneself and expect negative outcomes

(2) Higher trait neuroticism: being emotionally unstable, over-responsive to stress, and more likely to experience sadness, anxiety, anger, guilt, and so on

(3) Lower self-esteem: negative evaluation of one's worth

(4) Lower self-efficacy: lack of belief in one's ability

(5) Lower self-regulation capacity and poor emotion regulation skills: lack of knowledge of how to effectively regulate one's emotions

People with these psychological vulnerabilities are more likely to become passive in response to adverse events. They eventually give up active coping behavior, develop a state of learned helplessness and become depressed.

These psychological vulnerabilities are often caused by early-life stress or familial factors. For instance, children born to a depressed mother or a mother who became depressed postpartum have a roughly 400% increased risk of developing depression in their first 16 years of life and a lower IQ of 3-22 points (see Chapter 10).

In the 1960s, American psychiatrist Aaron Beck developed the cognitive therapy to change the vulnerability of negative inferential style in depressed patients. This cognitive therapy proves to be a major psychological therapy for patients with depression.

When Sadness Becomes Depression, Severe Cognitive Deficits Occur

Everyone has a time when he/she feels sad. Sickness, getting a B while expecting an A at school, failing an interview, missing someone, and losing something or somebody special all make people sad. Feeling sad, a negative mood in response to stress, is evolutionarily adaptive. It helps to direct attention to the problem causing the mood and facilitates problem-solving. Yet, when the negative mood is prolonged and sadness becomes depression, it becomes destructive.

Depression is not simply prolonged sadness. It is characterized by the loss of interest or pleasure in daily activities. People with depression may experience significant weight loss or gain, develop insomnia or hypersomnia, display a lack of energy (or fatigue), possess an inability to concentrate and think, and develop feelings of worthlessness or excessive guilt and recurrent thoughts of death.

Contrary to the positive mood, negative mood narrows people's attention. The narrowed attention filters out important information from higher level processing by the brain and impairs people's cognitive ability. In 2013, psychologist Hannah Snyder performed a meta-analysis synthesizing 113 previous studies and found that patients with depression showed severe deficits on every aspect of executive function, including inhibitory control, cognitive flexibility, and working memory. This reduced executive function induces broad cognitive failures in everyday life, such as poorer academic achievement, lower workplace performance, and more driving accidents.

Sadly, the compromised executive function in individuals with depression impairs their problem-solving ability. On the one hand, it induces more chronic stress, and on the other hand, it impairs people's emotion regulation capacity and makes them more vulnerable to depression. The outcome is a further increased risk for depression, so it is another vicious circle. Because of the prevalence of chronic stress, the stability of psychological vulnerabilities over time, and the cognitive deficits shown by depressed people, depression as a mental disorder is rather prevalent but difficult to treat clinically:

(1) According to the World Mental Health Survey conducted in 17 countries, on average, about one in 20 people have an episode of depression in a one-year period.

(2) Depression often starts at a young age, typically during the teenage or early adult years. In any given year, about 20% of adolescents experience a mental health problem, most commonly depression or anxiety.

(3) Due to a lack of a solid neurobiological basis, current diagnosis and treatments for depression are not very successful. Only half of the patients with depression respond to clinical treatments. Among those who respond, roughly half nonetheless relapse within a year.

For these reasons, depression causes serious health and social problems. In 1996, the World Health Organization (WHO) ranked depression the fourth leading cause of disability worldwide and projected that it would be the second by 2020. Strikingly, however, by 2000 depression had already become the leading cause of disability.

Students with High Depressive Symptoms Perform Poorly at School

Several longitudinal studies have followed adolescents throughout their high school years. The results consistently showed that depression was associated with reduced academic achievement in many subjects such as math, geography, history, chemistry, and biology. Specifically:

(1) Higher levels of depressive symptoms were correlated with concurrent poorer academic performance;

(2) An increase in depressive symptoms from one semester to the next semester or from one grade to the next grade was associated with a dramatic decrease in academic performance;

(3) Those that had consistently high levels of depressive symptoms throughout the high school years were more likely to have the lowest academic achievement;

(4) Adolescents who had a depressed friend, regardless of their own depressive symptoms, were less likely to be involved in academic activities (e.g., paying attention to what the teachers are saying during classes), showed lower willingness to devote effort to mastering academic skills, and enjoyed school less.

This underlies the educational issues raised by depression, as depressive symptoms are popular in students. A 2002 WHO survey showed that globally on average, one in four high school students reported depressive symptoms on a weekly basis, with the highest symptoms being among older and female students. A 2015 Canadian survey of high school students showed that roughly one out of three adolescents had depressive symptoms that remained moderate or elevated across their high school years.

As Little as 10-29 Minutes of Daily Exercise Prevents the Onset of Depression

Depression is driven by chronic stress and psychological vulnerabilities. As we have seen earlier, exercise reduces stress. Physiologically, regular exercise reduces stress response and enhances neurogenesis, which protects the brain and enhances problem-solving abilities. Psychologically, regular exercise changes psychological vulnerabilities: it increases self-esteem, self-efficacy, and self-regulation capacity.

Thus, epidemiological studies consistently report a protective effect of exercise on depression. Individuals who exercise more have less depressive symptoms and are less likely to be diagnosed with depression in their later years. In a 10-year longitudinal study, Michel Lucas at Harvard University found that as little as 10-29 minutes of daily exercise, such as walking, jogging, running, bicycling, playing tennis, lap swimming, yoga, dance, lawn mowing, and so on, were preventive in the onset of depression. Higher levels of daily exercise were associated with further decreased risk of developing depression over the 10-year period.

Exercise as a Potent Therapy

Regular exercise increases the levels of neurotrophic factors such as BDNF and promotes neurogenesis. Both the levels of BDNF and neurogenesis are decreased in patients with depression. Thus, for individuals already diagnosed with depression, exercise exerts powerful therapeutic effects.

Just like those who played Pokémon Go to capture characters reported better moods, patients with depression report an improved mood after increasing their daily exercise. In a one-week-long study, Jutta Mata at Stanford University gave each participant (with or without depression) a hand-held personal digital assistant (PDA). Through the PDA, she prompted the participants randomly eight times per day and asked them to answer questions about their affective states and physical activities. As expected, participants with depression reported lower positive affect and higher negative affect than those never-depressed healthy participants. Nevertheless, for both healthy participants and participants with depression, positive affect increased from a prompt after an inactive period to a later prompt at which exercise (such as walking, yoga, tennis, running, and basketball) was reported. Positive affect also increased from days without exercise to days with exercise. Furthermore, patients with depression, in particular, showed a dose-response effect: longer duration, higher intensity of exercise increased their positive affect more than shorter duration, lower intensity of exercise.

Exercise as a clinical therapy is potent in treating depression, especially for patients with mild or moderate symptoms. The *Cochrane Database of Systematic Reviews*, a leading resource for systematic reviews in health care, recently published a meta-analysis of randomly controlled trials. The therapeutic effect of exercise training on depression was comparable to psychological and pharmacological treatments. In this meta-analysis, a dose-dependent effect also occurred. The longer duration of exercise training, the bigger the antidepressant effect. Whereas an effect size of 0.42 was observed for training with 1-12 sessions, it increased to 0.70 and 0.80 when the training lasted for 13-24 sessions and 25-36 sessions respectively.

～～～

CHAPTER 9
Exercise as Medicine: People Who Exercise Regularly Sleep More Soundly

If sleep does not serve an absolutely vital function, then it is the biggest mistake the evolutionary process ever made.

— Allan Rechtschaffen & Anthony Kales, *A Manual of Standardized Terminology, Techniques and Scoring System for Sleep Stages of Human Subjects* (1968)

In 1965, to gain an entry into the Guinness Book of World Records, a 17-year old San Diego high school student named Randy Gardner decided to attempt to stay awake continuously for 264 hours. Gardner's parents were concerned about the effect of the experiment on their son. His father, a career military officer, asked a navy doctor to track Gardner's condition. Two friends of Gardner's took alternating shifts to keep him awake with activities such as television and basketball. For the first day, Gardner was able to remain awake with no prompting, but things quickly went bad. He soon lost his ability to concentrate and repeat simple tongue twisters. His speech became slow and fragmented. He found it difficult to name common objects. He also became moody, irritable, and uncooperative. On day 11, when asked to subtract seven from one-hundred, Gardner made it to 65 after five subtractions and stopped: he had forgotten what he was supposed to do.

Sleep is important for normal cognitive and emotional functioning. Since Gardner's experiment, psychologists have used many experimental tasks to quantify the effects of sleep deprivation on people's cognitive abilities. In a typical experimental setting, psychologists asked subjects to stay awake without sleeping for a consecutive 24 to 48 hours period. After that, they asked the subjects to perform various cognitive tasks. The subjects' performance was compared to control subjects who had slept as they wanted or for 7-8 hours. In 2010, Julian Lim and David Dinges at the University of Pennsylvania performed a meta-analysis of 147 cognitive tests published in 70 articles using the above experimental setting. Lim and Dinges concluded that 24-48 hours of sleep deprivation had a dramatic deleterious effect on every aspect of executive function and short-term memory.

When deprived of sleep, people are poorer at detecting a single visual or auditory stimulus, slower to indicate the color of "RED" written in green or blue, and less flexible at thinking in different dimensions. When performing a cognitive task, sleep deprived individuals easily get distracted because of their decreased working memory. They can only hold limited information in their mind. They are also less accurate at recalling the information they came across tens of minutes earlier. Given the substantial detrimental effects of sleep deprivation, no wonder Randy Gardner forgot what he was supposed to do after 11 days of sleep loss: he had to store that in his memory.

In our everyday life, rather than a straight 24-48 hours of sleep deprivation, insufficient, poor sleep and chronic sleep deficiency are more common. We all have the experience that little sleep or poor sleep quality the previous night makes us sleepy and less efficient during the next day's work or study. Furthermore, people often sleep longer on weekends and non-workdays than work days. For instance, a recent survey shows that nurses get on average 84 minutes more sleep on non-work days than workdays. This suggests that people are not getting enough sleep on workdays and trying to "catch up" on non-workdays. Sleep loss is cumulative. By the end of a workweek, the influence of sleep loss is significant enough to impair people's learning and decision-making abilities. Indeed, it has been estimated that people's performance on tests related to attention and serial mathematical calculations is equally affected by 24 hours of total sleep loss and one week of getting only five hours of sleep per night.

Sleep Is Necessary for Memory

A breakthrough was made in the past two to three decades in the field of memory. That is, sleep is essential for the transformation of short-term memory into long-term memory. Specifically, a process of this transformation called system consolidation is sleep-dependent. In 1994, Matthew Wilson and Bruce McNaughton, two neuroscientists at the University of Arizona, recorded hippocampal place cells in rats during spatial behavioral tasks in which they learned to find paths leading to food. Wilson and McNaughton found that cells that fired together when the rat stayed at particular locations in the environment showed an increased tendency to fire together during later sleep. Other neuroscientists replicated this finding and showed that during sleep, especially the slow wave sleep, the neural circuits in the hippocampus were reactivated, and within 50 milliseconds of this reactivation, extrahippocampal areas including the prefrontal, parietal, visual cortex, and the striatum showed similar neural activity. The hippocampus encodes the spatiotemporal information of episodic events and sends the information to extrahippocampal areas, especially the prefrontal cortex for system consolidation during sleep. In particular, two major processes of system consolidation are supported by sleep: assimilation and abstraction.

Assimilation refers to integrating newly encoded memory information into preexisting knowledge networks and schemas. The newly encoded memory is more stable and resistant to decay.

Abstraction refers to a process in which rules and regularities are extracted from multiple memory representations to eventually form a more generalized schema in long-term memory. The original memory learned is decontextualized and generalized, so it can be applied independently from their specific spatiotemporal context during acquisition. Subsequent sleep, notably the rapid eye movement (REM) sleep, helps to stabilize the newly transformed memory representation.

When asked to perform memory tasks, such as recalling episodes of events, facts, and discrimination of similar visual textures, subjects show a post-training improvement after a night's sleep, but not during an equal period of being awake. A night of high-quality sleep is a pre-requisite for learning.

Poor Sleep Induces Bad Moods

Recall Gardner's experiment. After staying awake for several days, he became moody, irritable, and uncooperative. Sleep not only is important for cognition, but also for mood regulation. People report more positive moods on days that followed better than usual quality of sleep. Furthermore, individuals with high sleep quality report more positive moods than individuals with poor sleep. In a 2016 survey of college freshmen, Shuzo Kumagai at Kyushu

University, Japan found that long sleep onset latency ($\geq$30 minutes), poor sleep quality and late bedtimes (later than 01:30) were associated with higher levels of depressive symptoms and suicidal ideation.

In line with these observations, insomnia is an important risk factor for depression. Insomnia is defined as difficulty in initiating and maintaining sleep, early morning awakening, and nonrestorative sleep (the feeling of not being refreshed after sleep). It is accompanied by decreased daytime functioning. Insomnia is increasingly recognized as a contributing factor to depression in all populations. In adults, a meta-analysis of longitudinal studies has estimated that insomnia increases the risk of subsequent depression by 160%. In adolescents, those with symptoms of insomnia are more likely to report various psychological problems including depression, anxiety, conduct disorders, eating disorders, and substance abuse. These adolescents meanwhile have more health problems and difficulty getting along with peers and family members.

Students with Poor Sleep Achieve Less at School

Sleep is highly associated with executive function, memory, and mood. Thus, sleep is essential for academic achievement as well. Students with insufficient amount of sleep or poor quality of sleep display diminished daytime alertness and more depressed mood. They are more likely to report worse grades at school. In one study of high school students, those who performed bad at school (got C, D, or F) reported on average about 25 minutes less sleep and went to bed 40 minutes later on school nights compared to students getting As and Bs. In another study of college students taking an introduction psychology course, those reporting poor sleep quality in the previous one-month period before the study got lower grades in the course and lower GPA for the academic term than those reporting good quality of sleep.

These observations deserve further attention since sleep problems are common among students. As reported by Shuzo Kumagai at Kyushu University in Japan, 23.4% of the freshmen showed long sleep onset latency ($\geq$30 mins), 33.3% had poor sleep quality, and 9.1% showed late bedtime (later than 01:30). A 2002 WHO survey showed that in children and adolescents, globally the average rate of morning sleepiness on a weekly basis was 40%.

Light-emitting Electronic Devices Cause Poor Sleep

One factor that may have contributed to this high prevalence of poor sleep in students is light-emitting electronic devices such as cell phones and tablets. Many have a habit of using cell phones or tablets for gaming or social networking service before bedtime. Using such devices before bedtime lengthens the sleep onset latency, delays the circadian clock, reduces the amount and delays the timing of REM sleep, and reduces alertness the next morning. Recently, it has been reported that high school students who text longer at night after lights are out sleep fewer hours, are sleepier during the day, and have lower academic achievement.

"The Only Way to Recover From Lost Sleep Is to Get More of It"

In his bestseller *Dreamland: Adventures in the Strange Science of Sleep*, David K. Randall told the story about the U.S. Defense Advanced Research Projects Agency spent millions of dollars trying to find a way for soldiers to go without sleep for one hundred hours and still perform well on common tasks. However, none of their tests worked. "No drug or procedure has been found to replicate and replace the benefits of sleep. It is unlikely that there ever will be,"

Randall wrote, "the only way to recover from lost sleep was to get more of it later."

How much sleep is necessary for us to maintain everyday optimal functioning? Generally, adults need about 7-9 hour of sleep per day. Teenagers need 8-10 hours of sleep. Children need 9-11 hours.

Obtaining enough sleep day-to-day obviously is important, but obtaining high-quality sleep is essential as well. Several specific strategies that help optimize sleep are presented below:

● Establish more regularity and consistency in the timing of daily activities, especially the timing of getting up, evening meals, and bedtime routine. For example, you may want to read, take a hot shower, and then go to bed. Higher levels of regularity in behavioral rhythms are associated with better sleep outcomes, lower depression, and improved health;

● Do not use light-emitting electronic devices such as cell phones and tablets before bedtime, as it has negative effects on sleep;

● Try to reduce total sitting time and time spent television viewing. Each extra hour per day of total sitting is associated with greater odds of poor sleep quality. Each extra hour per day of television viewing is associated with greater odds of long sleep onset latency (≥ 30 min), waking up too early in the morning, poor sleep quality, and high risk for obstructive sleep apnea;

● Perform aerobic exercise every day (evidence below). But try to avoid vigorous exercise within 2 hours of going to bed, as vigorous late-night exercise may produce increased arousal and prolong the sleep onset latency.

Regular Exercise Makes You Sleep More Soundly

At least five meta-analyses have been performed in adolescents, adults, older people, and people with sleep problems. In all these populations, regular exercise such as walking, cycling, treadmill, or Taichi shortens the sleep onset latency, improves sleep efficiency and sleep quality. They have fewer awakenings at night, feel more rested in the morning, and work more effectively during the daytime. Longer habits of exercise bring greater benefits.

In a recent randomized controlled trial, Juriena de Vries at Radboud University, The Netherlands, selected college students who were physically inactive (exercise less than one hour a week) and had high levels of study-related fatigue. de Vries randomly assigned these students into exercise or control groups. Students in the exercise group were asked to run outdoors three times a week for six weeks: two times of which they ran in a group of ten people under the supervision of a licensed running trainer and once independently (either with or without others). The running sessions were scheduled at 6 PM to 7 PM and consisted of 15 minutes of warming up (low-intensity running alternated with walking and flexibility exercises), 30 minutes of low-intensity running (in a pace that allowed them to have a conversation during running), and 15 minutes of cooling down. Six weeks later, compared to students in the control group, students in the exercise group showed more decrease in fatigue. Furthermore, only the students in the exercise group showed improvement in sleep quality and cognitive functioning. The students in the exercise group found it easier to fall asleep at night, were less likely to wake up during the night, and felt more refreshed after waking up. Meanwhile, they showed increased working memory capacity and decreased self-regulatory failures (i.e., ego depletion) over time. For instance, they became less likely to forget where they put things, people's names and appointments.

They were also less likely to daydream or have their minds wander during conversations, classes or meetings, to lose their temper, and to fail to notice signposts on the road.

~~~

CHAPTER 10
Why Exercising as a Family Provides the Most Benefits

Exercise with your child. It raises your child's IQ and self-regulation as well as your own. A win-win situation.

— Chong Chen

In Chapter 1, we introduced an American national survey of almost 12,000 high school students. In that study, relative to students frequently viewing television and videos, students who regularly exercised had higher academic achievements, smoked less, did more housework and part-time work outside of home. Among students who regularly exercised, those who exercised with their parents experienced the most benefits. They additionally showed reduced delinquency (violence, property damage), lower frequency of drinking and use of illegal drugs, and were more likely to get enough sleep each night. In other words, exercising with parents brought the most benefits, even more benefits than exercising alone or with friends. This finding was not serendipitous either. Recently, sports scientist Mehdi Kargarfard found similar results in Iran.

Kargarfard assigned 7-10th-grade female students to an afterschool exercise program. The program consisted of two 90-minute sessions of aerobic exercise and stretching per week for 12 weeks. Kargarfard randomly selected half of the students and asked them to invite their mothers to participate in the program together with them. Thus, in this study, half of the students attended the exercise program alone whereas the other half attended with their mothers. This seemingly subtle difference made a big impact 12 weeks later. Compared with those attending the program alone, the students who participated in the program with their mothers had more increases in fitness on almost every measurement after the program. They showed higher aerobic fitness as indexed by VO_2 max, higher abdominal muscle strength, and endurance in a sit-ups test. As expected, the students' mothers also showed improved fitness after the program. These findings suggest that exercising with parents brings more benefits than exercising alone. In this chapter, we will look at the underlying reasons for why this is the case.

Enriched Environment Promotes Brain Development

Canadian psychologist Donald Hebb was the Ph.D. supervisor of Brenda Milner, who observed the famous patient H.M. who lost his hippocampus in Chapter 4. Hebb is famous for his influential theory published in 1949 that "Neurons that fire together wire together." This theory excellently captures the mechanism of synaptic plasticity and forms the molecular basis of learning and memory. Two years before he published the theory, Hebb reported another anecdotal and pioneering observation. He found that rats that he took home as pets showed superior performance on problem-solving tests over rats raised in cages in the laboratory. To explain this phenomenon, he proposed the concept of "enriched environment." He argued that an enriched early environment, which gave an animal more physical and social stimulation, promoted behavioral development.

More than a decade later, in the early 1960s, Mark Rosenzweig at the University of California, Berkeley, brought the concept of the enriched environment into neuroscientific research. He compared rats raised alone in normal cages and those placed in cages with toys, ladders, tunnels, running wheels, or those that received daily handling and maze training in groups. He found the weight of the cerebral cortex was increased in these two latter groups of rats raised with more physical and social stimulation (i.e., an enriched environment). More detailed analysis showed that enriched environment was associated with an increased depth (thickness) of the cortex and greater numbers of synapse (by which neurons pass information to each other) and glia (non-neuronal cells which support neurons).

Subsequently, scientists have consistently found that an enriched environment increases serum levels of neurotrophic factors such as BDNF, promotes neurite branching and synapse formation in the cortex, and increases the density of synapses, dendritic spines (by which neurons receive information from other neurons), and neurogenesis in the hippocampus. Meanwhile, animals raised in an enriched environment have enhanced learning ability and superior memories. They also show lower levels of depression and anxiety-like behaviors. Interestingly, exercise alone, such as wheel or treadmill running, produces comparable beneficial effects on the brain and behavior in comparison to an enriched environment.

Families at High Social Economic Status Provide More Enriched Environments to Their Children

In his 2009 insightful book *Intelligence and how to get it: why schools and cultures count*, psychologist Richard Nisbett at the University of Michigan noticed a cognitive cultural difference between families at higher, middle, and low socioeconomic status (SES). This cognitive cultural difference accounts for the differences in the cognitive abilities of the children raised in these environments. The cognitive cultural difference is simply the difference in the degree of enrichment. High-SES parents tend to provide a more enriched environment for their children.

High-SES parents prepare their children for life early, cultivating their abilities for questioning and analytic minds from a young age. They talk to their children more often, bathe their children in words, with running commentaries about the surrounding world, about their own experiences, emotions, and ideas, and question the child concerning his or her needs and interests. They involve their children in dinner conversations, exposing the children to various vocabulary, information, and analytic thinking. They have more books and read books often to their children and at an early age. When reading, they try to elaborate on what is read in the book, make connections and explanations of the story, and relate it to the real world. They also encourage their children to talk and think about the story by asking them questions.

Low-SES parents talk less to their children; and when they talk, it is usually in the form of commands and orders with little cognitive involvement or stimulation to the children. They carry on discussions at the dinner table with the assumption that the children have nothing to do with it or no interest in participating. They have limited books at home and only sometimes may read to their children. However, during the reading, they seldom explain deeply about what is being read or connect it to the real world.

It is estimated that during interactions with their children, high-SES parents speak about 2000 words per hour to the children, whereas low-SES parents speak only about 1300. By the age of three, the children in the high-SES family have heard about 30 million words, compared to 20 million by their peers raised in the low-SES family. Middle-SES parents lie between the high and low-SES parents.

Interestingly, two studies published in the year 2015 made a further observation that parents with more income and high educational levels gave more support to their children for participating in sports. Their children exercised more often.

Given these cognitive environmental differences created by parenting behavior, their offspring show robustly different cognitive developments. Several adoption studies carried out in the U.S. and Europe have found that children raised in a high-SES family have IQs that are on average 12-18 points higher compared to those raised in a low-SES family. This holds true whether the biological mothers of the children are of high or low-SES. Furthermore, children raised in a high-SES family also have a higher capacity for self-regulation, and have less emotional and social problems such as depression, obesity, drug and alcohol abuse, violence, and criminality. The more enriched environment the high-SES family provides accounts for this superior development outcome.

Psychologically Healthy Parents Provide More Enriched Environments

The cognitive and mental health status of the parents also affects their parenting behavior and the development of their children. Parents with more stress, depression, anxiety, sleep problems, marital conflict, and low executive function and self-regulation capacity have children with worse cognitive and emotional development. Being more preoccupied with their own concerns and problems, parents under these conditions:

(1) Are less responsive to behaviors, communications and emotional expressions of the children;

(2) Spend less time in caregiving activities such as play and breastfeeding (for the mothers);

(3) Show decreased acceptance, warmth, encouragement, and nurturance, poor parent-child relationship, increased hostility, harsh or inconsistent discipline, lack of parental support and involvement in school, more punishment or abuse of their child, and more household chaos (e.g., homes that are less structured, more crowded, noisy).

These parenting behaviors are detrimental to the healthy development of the children and eventually cause deficits in cognition and self-regulation. For instance, it has been reported that compared to their peers with non-depressed mothers, children, especially boys, born to depressed mothers or mothers who became depressed postpartum have lower IQs of 3-22 points and lower academic scores of about 10% points at school. They also have a roughly 400% increased risk of being diagnosed with depression in their first 16 years of life. (I'm writing a series "Your Baby's Developing Brain" on how parents can build an enriched environment for the baby during pregnancy and after birth. If you're interested, please feel free to sign up for my newsletter at http://brainandlife.net.)

Exercising as a Family: Building an Enriched Environment for Both the Parents and Children

Given the above observations, we can now fully appreciate the benefits of exercising as a family. The most important and exciting point about exercising as a family is that, exercise is an enriched environment for not only the children but also their parents, who themselves are the most important environmental factors to their children.

As we have shown throughout this book, regular exercise improves executive function, enhances memory, boosts positive mood, buffers stress, promotes the capacity for self-regulation, reduces negative emotions, and improves sleep quality. All these benefits hold true for both children and adults. Thus, exercising as a family forms an enriched environment for both the child and the parents.

Parents with more stress, depression, anxiety, sleep problems, and low executive function and self-regulation capacity are too occupied with their own life concerns to pay enough attention and care for their children. Participating in exercise with their children can improve all these conditions of the parents. It promotes the parenting ability of the parents and helps them establish a more enriched environment for their children.

Besides, exercising as a family has three other benefits. First, it improves marital satisfaction and promotes closeness and acceptance of the couples. In a 2004 study, James W. Carson at the University of North Carolina adapted a couple-based yoga program.

In this program, couples did partner-incorporated versions of yoga, in which they facilitated one another with yoga postures. They were also trained to be more aware of their shared experiences with their partner and developed a new understanding of their relationships. Carson found that eight weekly 2.5 hours of the program not only improved the individual partners' optimism, relaxation, and reduced their distress, but also enhanced their satisfaction with their partners, promoted closeness, acceptance of one another and reduced relationship distress.

Second, playing and interacting with children itself is a parenting activity. It promotes communication between the children and parents and forms another enriched environment for the children. This is especially important considering the fact that nowadays, people are too busy with work to find shared time with their children.

Third, it helps the child establish exercise as a habit, which assures the continuous benefits of exercise. When participating in exercise with parents, children feel more supported by their parents. This encourages them to engage in more exercise. As reported by several studies, the physical activity level of the parents is positively associated with that of their child's. When the child is at 3-5 years old, the physical activity level of parents explains 37.2% of the interpersonal difference in the child's physical activity level. As the child grows older, parents' support towards the child's exercise becomes more important than the parents' physical activity *per se*, because now the child has established exercise as a habit and participate in exercise more often with friends. Still, at 10-14 years old, parents' physical activity level and support for their children to take part in physical activity together explain 41% of the interpersonal difference in their children's physical activity level. Here, parental support takes many forms:

(1) Encouraging the child to exercise

(2) Praising the child for his effort to exercise

(3) Buying exercise or sports equipment for the child

(4) Providing transportations for the child to attend exercise or sports

(5) Watching the child play

(6) Teaching/training the child how to play sports

(7) Exercising or playing sports with the child or as a family

Given these benefits, now we can understand the observation we introduced at the beginning of this chapter. Children exercising with their parent(s) benefit more than those who participate in school-based exercise or exercise alone.

If you are a parent, exercise with your child regularly. Meanwhile, practice (and teach your child to practice) any strategies that have been proven effective in increasing positive moods, reducing stress and depression, improving quality of sleep, and enhancing executive function and self-regulation. It raises your child's intelligence and self-regulation as well as your own. A win-win situation for all involved.

~~~

CHAPTER 11
Exercise Is the Key to Optimal Aging

A happy old age requires both physical health and mental health. For mental health, love is necessity. So is being alive. So is being able to think straight. We need physical and cognitive competence to build the social surrounds that give us love and support later on, and it is love and support that encourage us to care for ourselves well and keep ourselves healthy, even when the going gets rough.

— Harvard psychiatrist George Vaillant, *Triumphs of Experience: The Men of the Harvard Grant Study* (2012)

My first in-depth exposure to the concept of aging society was in 2011. I was spending a year studying psychiatric epidemiology in Professor Hiko Tamashiro's Department of Global Health and Epidemiology at Hokkaido University. Before coming to Hokkaido University, Professor Tamashiro has long worked at the WHO (Geneva) on public health issues. Since the year 2009, Tamashiro, helped by epidemiologist Asuna Arai and Yoshi Obayashi, has established *The Consortium for Global Health Research, Education, and Training*. The consortium comprised researchers from eight institutes from Asia, American, and Europe. Since its establishment, the Consortium has regularly held conferences in Sapporo, Peradeniya, Seoul and other places. In the year 2011, the Consortium held *The Second International Graduate School Intensive Course on Aging Society and Sustainable Development* in Sapporo. I was one attendant of the intensive course. During the course, lecturers introduced the status, challenges of and potential solutions for the aging society from different disciplines including policy-making, medicine, engineering, artificial intelligence, and so on. Attendants, in collaborative working groups, were asked to propose solutions to solve a specific issue.

This intensive course drew my attention to issues surrounding aging. We are now in a highly aging society. Because of better nutrition and medical development, people live longer. This increase in life expectancy causes the aging of populations: the proportion of people aged 65 years and older becomes increasingly larger. Take Japan, the country with the highest aging rate, for example. In 2000, the proportion of people aged 65 years and older was 16.7%, which means one in six persons was an elderly person. In the year 2010, it increased to 22.7%, which means one in five persons was an elderly person. When I was writing this paragraph, the proportion had again risen to 26.7% in the year 2015, which means one in four persons is an elderly person. It is further predicted that by the year 2035, 33.4% or one in three persons is an elderly person. This high aging process raises many economic and social issues.

Economically, young and middle-aged adults (working population) have to work to support the elderly, as the elderly retire after a certain age, for instance 60 years old. This produces a big economic burden to the working population. In 1990, it was estimated that 5.8 working-age persons were supporting one elderly person; in 2000, 2010 and 2015, this figures changed to 3.9, 2.8, and 2.3 respectively. It has been further estimated that the figure will become 1.3 by the year 2050. One solution my collaborative working group at the intensive course proposed for this issue was to raise the statutory retirement age, for data shows that most of the elderly people aged 60 to 69 are still healthy (in good physical and cognitive functions) and wish to continue their work. Indeed, a recent trend worldwide is to increase this statutory retirement age. For instance, Germany and the U.K. are said to be planning to raise the age from 65 to 67.

Yet, a considerable proportion of the elderly is bogged down with health problems. According to the 2013 *Comprehensive Survey of Living Conditions* carried out by the Japanese Ministry of Health, Labour and Welfare, 15% of the Japanese people aged 65-69, 20% aged 70-74, 27% aged 75-79, 37% aged 80-84, and 47% aged 85 and above suffer from health conditions that affect normal daily life and working. In the year 2012, 15% of the Japanese people aged 65 and above have dementia (one in seven persons), which is estimated to rise to 20% (one in five persons) in the year 2025 and 34.3% (one in three persons) in the year 2060.

The Concept of Successful Aging: Some People Age Well While Others Do Not

Scientists have long been asking what makes the difference between the two groups of older adults; one group ages well while the other not so well? In 1961, in an editorial in the first issue of *The Gerontologist*, Robert Havighurst introduced the term "successful aging" to the scientific community. He argued that the goal of the science of gerontology is to increase enjoyment and satisfaction during this later stage of life. To achieve such a goal, it is essential to have a theory of successful aging. He called upon the young field of gerontology to study and promote successful aging. But this proves to be a difficult task, for it involves multi-dimensional definition which comprises biological, physical, cognitive, emotional, and social components. After developing the biopsychosocial model of medicine in the 1970s, biological and psychosocial concepts have finally been incorporated into the models of successful aging.

In a landmark paper published in the journal *Science* in 1987, John Rowe and Robert Kahn distinguished between successful, usual, and pathological aging. Pathological aging is associated with enhanced cognitive decline, increased rates of injury, hospitalization, dependence on assisted living and mortality. Usual aging functions well, but with a high risk for disease and disability. Successful aging shows a high level of function across several domains, and most importantly:

(1) Free of disease and disability

(2) High physical and cognitive functioning

(3) Engagement in social and productive activities

Longitudinal studies have indicated that executive function declines after age 55, whereas episodic memory performance remains relatively stable until about 60-65 years old, after which an accelerated decline is typically observed. This comes with reduced volume of the hippocampus and prefrontal cortex, and reduced adult neurogenesis and BDNF levels in the hippocampus. Specifically, the annual decline of the volume of the hippocampus is estimated to be 1-2% in non-demented older adults and 3-5% for individuals with mild cognitive impairment or Alzheimer's disease. Alzheimer's disease is the most prevalent form of dementia, characterized by progressive episodic memory loss and other executive, linguistic, and behavioral symptoms. Yet, it has also been observed that in about 10% of people older than 70 years old, their cognitive performance is relatively preserved and their hippocampal volume is relatively stable. This 10% of aged people has been categorized as meeting the criterion for successful cognitive aging.

A typical example of such a person with successful aging was well demonstrated in the 2015 American comedy film *"The Intern."* In this film, the seventy-year-old widower Ben, a retired executive, applied to a senior citizen intern program of an e-commerce fashion startup after retirement. A typical old-day gentleman, he was healthy, positive, active and regularly did Taichi. The film described how he developed peaceful and good relationships with people in the company, and how he used his wisdom, knowledge, and experience to help the founder and CEO Jules in her work and family life.

Yet, Rowe and Kahn's model of successful aging is criticized because it only captures the outcome of aging. It didn't mention any processes of how to achieve a better outcome. Besides, the usage of the word "successful" excludes a considerable proportion of people bothered by physical or cognitive symptoms. Rather than "successful aging," I prefer the term "optimal aging" as the aging process of all elderly people can be improved and optimized.

Fitness at College Predicts Optimal Aging Over 60 Years Later

Several other vivid examples of optimal aging can be found in the 2012 book *Triumphs of Experience: The Men of the Harvard Grant Study* by Harvard psychiatrist George Vaillant. Begun in 1938, the Harvard Grant Study followed the physical and emotional health of over 200 Harvard college men, starting with their undergraduate days, until now, who (those still alive) are in their nineties. George Vaillant, a previous director of this study, gave many detailed descriptions of those who eventually achieved optimal aging, although with different life trajectories. Here, optimal aging was defined by Vaillant as ten events or achievements, primarily based on Rowe and Kahn's model:

(1) Included in *Who's Who in America* (a publication containing short biographies of distinguished Americans, Vaillant noted that 21% of the men had been included)

(2) Earning income in the study's top quartile

(3) Low in psychological distress

(4) Success and enjoyment in work, marriage, and play since age 65

(5) Good subjective health at age 75

(6) Good subjective and objective physical and mental health at age 80

(7) Being actively involved in empathic nurturing of a new generation, especially adolescents and adults other than one's own children

(8) Availability of social supports other than one's wife and kids between ages 60 and 75

(9) In a good marriage between ages 60 and 85

(10) Close to one's children between ages 60 and 75

Filling up what was lacking in Rowe and Kahn's model, in this study, Vaillant analyzed what variables that were collected at a young age could predict optimal aging at age 60-80 that he defined. He put all the data available from college up to midlife into the statistical analysis, including those physical, psychological, and social data directly measured at college, from interviews with the men and their parents, wives, and children. Vaillant found that fitness at college, as measured by athletic prowess and treadmill endurance, is one of the most significant factors that predicted optimal aging. Those with higher fitness throughout college aged better over 60 years later than their less fit classmates. What makes fitness so important is the habit of exercise, which builds strength and endurance. Those with higher fitness levels during college exercised regularly at college and throughout their whole lives. It was this habit that won them better aging. Additionally, several other factors were also significant in predicting optimal aging, including a warm childhood, good childhood temperament, positivity at college (full of energy, cheerfulness), college soundness (good at handling problems they might confront), mature psychological coping style at age 20-35, and warm adult relationships at age 30-45. Interestingly, as we have seen throughout this present book, regular exercise by the parents and the child contributes to most of the above factors that predict optimal aging.

Exercise Is the Only Intervention Consistently Demonstrated to Attenuate Functional Decline in Older People

In 2015, Stephen Anton and 34 other scientists across the medical sciences at the University of Florida published an article titled *"Successful Aging: Advancing the Science of Physical Independence in Older Adults."* They noted that the mobility performance as measured by walking speed appears to be an excellent surrogate marker of overall health. Walking speed predicts the maintenance of physical independence, a cornerstone of successful aging. Walking speed is frequently measured based on the time to complete a distance ranging from 4 meters to 400 meters or the distance covered within a pre-specified period, typically 6 minutes. Accumulating evidence indicates that slow walking speeds and reductions in walking speed strongly predict functional decline, major health outcomes, and mortality in older adults. Specifically, <1 meter/second indicates a high risk and < 0.8 meter/second indicates a very high risk. Even small improvements in walking speed, such as >0.05 meter/second, have been found to translate to meaningful improvements in the performance of activities in daily life such as stair climbing and walking a block.

This reminds me of Professor Akito Kawaguchi at Hokkaido University Faculty of Education. He is tall, thin, who walks fast. In March of 2012, Professor Akito Kawaguchi (then 63 years old, although still quite young) and Professor Masao Mizuno visited Peking University Health Science Center, with me being the translator for them. Besides Peking University, we also went to the Great Wall and Temple of Heaven for sightseeing. It impressed me that throughout our journey, Professor Kawaguchi walked far ahead of us so he had to stop and wait for us to catch up often.

In their paper, Anton and his 34 co-authors reviewed available interventions to enhance physical function and mobility, including lifestyle (diet) intervention, exercise, cognitive training, non-invasive brain stimulation, pharmaceutical interventions, nutritional supplements, hormone supplementation, and the use of smart and connected technologies. After an extensive review of the literature, they concluded that:

"To date, physical exercise is the only intervention consistently demonstrated to attenuate functional decline among older adults."

This conclusion holds true for physical, cognitive, emotional, and social functions. The breadth of the benefits of exercise is impressive. For instance, there are many social and emotional factors that are associated with physical and cognitive functions in the elderly, and which are all positively affected by exercise.

(1) A longitudinal study involving almost 2,000 people aged 70-89 years found that individuals in the upper 25th percentile of academic and career achievements showed better cognitive function with a delay of cognitive impairment by 8.7 years, as compared to those in the lower 25th percentile;

(2) Optimism, self-efficacy, a sense of personal control over memory and cognition, and more positive emotions are related to better physical and cognitive functioning in the elderly;

(3) High levels of chronic stress or daily stress are associated with more rapid cognitive decline and everyday memory problems later in life;

(4) Hostile attitudes and ineffective stress coping skills at a young age increase the risk for experiencing cognitive problems decades later;

(5) Living a lonely life, high levels of depressive mood and neuroticism, and increases in anxiety in late adulthood are associated with an enhanced decline of physical and cognitive functioning;

(6) Poor sleep in middle-age is linked to neurodegeneration-related biomarkers (e.g., amyloid deposition) and later cognitive decline; sleep disturbances such as difficulty falling asleep and frequent awakening is associated with physical and cognitive impairment in older adults;

(7) Suffering from a vascular disease is associated with increased risk for Alzheimer's disease;

(8) Obesity contributes to cognitive decline and increases the risk of dementia (see Chapter 12).

In 2003, psychologists Stanley Colcombe and Arthur Kramer performed a meta-analysis of eighteen exercise intervention studies in older people aged 55-80 published between 1966 and 2001. They concluded that exercise training effectively improves executive function in this population. They also found several moderators of the effect:

(1) A combination of aerobic with resistance exercise is more effective than aerobic exercise in isolation;

(2) Long-term training (> 6 months) is more effective than short and medium-term training;

(3) For each session, moderate (31-45 min) and long (46-60 min) sessions are more effective than short ones (15-30 min);

(4) Training groups with more females (> 50% female) are more effective than those with more males.

Exercise Reverses Aging-Induced Brain Loss

As we have seen in Chapter 3, the improvement in cognitive functions in older people is associated with an increase in hippocampal volume. In the 2011 study by Kirk Erickson, 40 minutes of moderate-intensity aerobic exercise training three sessions a week for one year increased aerobic fitness by 7.8% in adults aged 55-80. Aerobic fitness typically declines 8-10% per age decade in healthy adults and 20-30% per decade in healthy people over 70 years. This 7.8% increase in aerobic fitness itself is exciting. One year of aerobic exercise can effectively reverse almost one decade of aging-induced decrease in fitness.

Meanwhile, the improvement in aerobic fitness is associated with increases in hippocampal volume and improvements in spatial memory. Across the one-year period, people who engaged in the aerobic training showed an overall 2% increase in the volume of the hippocampus. In control older adults who did not participate in the training, the hippocampal volume decreased by 1.4%. It suggests that one year of aerobic exercise reversed aging-related hippocampal loss in volume by more than two years.

Enriched Environment for the Elderly

Consistent with its profound role in raising children, an enriched environment is also the key to optimal aging. Hundreds of studies have provided compelling evidence that regular intellectual or cognitive engagement, meaningful social engagement, and maintaining a physically active lifestyle promote optimal aging, predict better maintenance of cognitive functioning and is associated with a reduced risk of developing dementia later in life. Examples of cognitively and socially engaging activities are:

(1) Reading books

(2) Attending plays

(3) Attending college courses

(4) Learning a foreign language

(5) Playing musical instruments

(6) Playing chess or bridge

(7) Painting or drawing

(8) Woodworking

(9) Writing for pleasure

(10) Doing volunteer work

(11) Going to church or temple

(12) Various other cultural activities

~~~

CHAPTER 12
Exercise for Losing Weight

Obesity is a double victory for consumerism. Instead of eating little, which will lead to economic contraction, people eat too much and then buy diet products - contributing to economic growth twice over.

— Israeli historian Yuval Noah Harari, *Sapiens: A Brief History of Humankind* (2014)

In November 2016, Canadian scientist Tauseef Khan and John Sievenpiper published a review paper on *European Journal of Nutrition*. They suggested that "sugar-sweetened beverages are a marker of an unhealthy lifestyle." They gave abundant evidence that fructose-containing sugars lead to weight gain and increase the risk for cardiovascular diseases and diabetes. Recall that self-regulation involves a limited capacity and depends on the level of blood glucose. Intake of sweetened beverages has been listed as a strategy to boost self-regulation and reverse ego depletion. Thus sugar is a double-edged sword in regards to the obesity epidemic.

According to WHO, worldwide 39% of adults aged 18 and over were overweight in 2014, and 13% were obese. That is, worldwide at least one in two people is overweight or obese. For adults, overweight and obesity are defined as follows:

Overweight is a $25 \leq BMI < 30$;

Obesity is a $BMI \geq 30$.

Here body mass index (BMI) is a simple index of weight-for-height that is commonly used to classify overweight and obesity in adults. It is defined as a person's weight in kilograms divided by the square of his/her height in meters (kg/m^2). Overweight and obesity are excessive fat accumulation due to excessive energy intake compared to calories consumed, especially from high-fat and high-carbohydrate foods. Sugar-sweetened beverages are typical examples of drinks with high calories.

Overweight and obesity increase oxidative stress and promote inflammation through the production of pro-inflammatory cytokines produced in adipose tissue. Overweight and obesity also increase the level of the stress hormone cortisol and produce a state of chronic stress in the body. The outcome is a dramatic increase in risks for many diseases, including cardiovascular diseases (e.g., heart disease, stroke), metabolic syndrome, type 2 diabetes, musculoskeletal disorders (especially osteoarthritis, a highly disabling degenerative disease of the joints), and cancers (including endometrial, breast, ovarian, prostate, liver, gallbladder, kidney, and colon). Perhaps more strikingly less known, overweight and obesity cause serious damage to the brain, which induces severe cognitive deficits and mental health problems.

Being Overweight and Obese Accelerate Brain Aging

Overweight and obesity increase the level of the stress hormone cortisol and produce a state of chronic stress in the body. As we have seen in Chapter 6, continuously high levels of cortisol damage and kill neurons, reduce the amount of neurotrophic factors and inhibit the creation of new neurons. As a result, being overweight and obese accelerate brain aging.

In a 2016 study, Lisa Ronan at the University of Cambridge found that overweight and obese people had an average of ten years increased brain age compared to their biological age. Using magnetic resonance imaging, Ronan examined the whole brain white matter volume of over 500 healthy individuals aged 20-87 years. White matter comprises neuronal projections (axons), which connects gray matter areas (the locations of neuronal cell bodies) and forms synapses. Synapses are the structural basis of all forms of learning and memory. Confirming the influence of aging, Ronan found that white matter in the cortex increased to peak level during the middle-aged years, around 40 years old, and decreased after that.

40 years of age were also an important fork for lean (BMI < 25) versus overweight (25 ≤ BMI < 30) and obese (BMI ≥ 30) individuals. Before 40 years, the white matter volume differences in these subjects were subtle. However, after 40 years, the differences became increasingly significant: overweight and obese subjects had a reduced white matter volume. Specifically, at 50 years of age, overweight and obese subjects had an estimated white matter volume of 445 cm^3 whereas lean subjects reached the same volume at an average age of 60 years. This difference persisted well past 80 years of age. In other words, overweight and obese subjects on average had a brain age ten years higher than their actual biological age.

That is not to say, however, that the brains of overweight and obese people before 40 years of age are healthy. In one study included subjects as young as 17-year old, overweight and obese individuals had a smaller whole brain volume than lean individuals. In another study involving 12-21 year old subjects, overweight and obese individuals had a smaller orbital frontal cortex, a part of the prefrontal cortex that is important for decision-making.

Overweight and Obesity Induce Broad Cognitive and Emotional Deficits

Because of the smaller brain, compared to individuals with a healthy weight, overweight and obese individuals often perform worse on tests of executive function and short-term memory. They tend to be poorer at inhibiting habitual responses and switching thinking in different dimensions and levels. They hold less information in their mind. After learning new information, they tend to forget at a faster rate. In line with this, overweight and obese children often perform poorly at school. Sports scientist Keita Kamijo at Waseda University, Japan reported that in children aged 7-9 years, those with higher BMI and fat mass (measured by dual X-ray absorptiometry) have lower academic achievement scores in reading, spelling, and arithmetic. In adults, obesity is related to over 280% higher risk of developing dementia 30 years later.

Being overweight and obese are also associated with many emotional, psychosomatic, and social problems.

(1) Due to body dissatisfaction and lower perceived self-competence, overweight and obesity are associated with low self-esteem in children and adolescents.

(2) Meta-analytic studies have estimated that obesity increases the risk of depression by 55%, and anxiety by 40%.

(3) They cause poor sleep. On the one hand, obesity is a well-known risk factor for the sleep disorder obstructive sleep apnea. On the other hand, obese individuals are more likely to report sleep disturbance, insomnia, and daytime sleepiness.

(4) Overweight and obese children are more likely to be both victims and perpetrators of peer aggression, in the form of name-calling, teasing, hitting, kicking, pushing, spreading rumors or lies, and so on.

Given the high prevalence of overweight and obesity, these detrimental outcomes of obesity posit serious social and educational issues.

To Lose Weight: Dietary Restriction

Overweight and obesity are the results of excessive energy intake compared to calories consumed, especially from high-fat and high-carbohydrate foods. Exercise and dietary restriction are two keys to losing excessive fat and keeping a healthy weight. Both are effective at reducing weight whereas a combination of both achieves the biggest effect.

Although the total calories a person needs each day varies depending on age, sex, height, weight, and physical activity level, it is frequently observed that reducing energy intake by 500-750 kcal/day effectively leads to weight loss in overweight and obese people. The most effective diet is to restrict energy intake from carbohydrates or fat, as suggested by a 2014 meta-analysis performed by Stanford scientist Edward J. Mills. Mills analyzed data from 48 randomized controlled trials and found that compared to no diet, the largest weight loss was associated with low-carbohydrate diets and low-fat diets.

For low-carbohydrate diets, carbohydrates comprised ≤ 40% of calorie intake (in kcal), protein comprised 30%, and fat comprised 30-55%.

For low-fat diets, carbohydrates comprised 60% of calorie intake, protein comprised 10-15%, and fat comprised ≤ 20%.

Mills found that low-carbohydrate diets led to 8.73 and 7.25 kg weight loss at sixth and twelfth month follow-up after an average of six months of intervention, respectively. Low-fat diets led to 7.99 and 7.27 kg weight loss at the sixth and twelfth month mark, respectively. The median age of the subjects was 45.7 years, median weight 94.1 kg, and median BMI 33.7.

Here, it has to be noted that low-fat diets are directed towards limiting energy intake from saturated fat. Whereas saturated fat such as fatty beef, pork, butter, and cheese posits risk to health, unsaturated fat including monounsaturated fat (such as those from olive oil, peanut oil, nuts) and polyunsaturated fat (such as those from fish, soybean, nuts) are health promoting. For instance, an omega-3 polyunsaturated fatty acids enriched diet (such as oily fish, e.g., salmon) increases serum levels of neurotrophic factors including BDNF and hippocampal neurogenesis, which contributes to enhanced cognitive functions.

One such low-saturated and high-unsaturated fat diet is the Mediterranean-style diet, which has been highly recommended by the scientific community. The Mediterranean-style diet is composed of the traditional dietary practices of countries bordering the Mediterranean Sea. It is characterized by:

(1) High intake of plant foods: vegetables, fruits, legumes, and cereals

(2) High intake of olive oil as the principal source of monounsaturated fat but low intake of saturated fat such as butter

(3) Moderate intake of fish

(4) Low to moderate consumption of dairy products

(5) Low consumption of meat and poultry

(6) Wine consumed in low to moderate amounts

Studies involving millions of people have consistently reported that high adherence to Mediterranean-style diet is associated with a healthier body weight, better cognitive functions and slower cognitive decline in aged people, a reduced risk of overweight and obesity, cardiovascular diseases, cancer, and Parkinson's and Alzheimer's diseases.

Exercise Leads to Additional Weight Loss

There are at least three reasons one should combine exercise with diet to lose weight. First, exercise leads to additional weight loss compared to dietary restriction alone, especially in the long-term. In the above 2014 meta-analysis, Mills found that including exercise as an add-on strategy led to an additional weight loss of 0.64 kg at the sixth month follow-up and 2.13 kg at the twelfth month follow-up. Because weight loss by dietary restriction often decreases as time passes after the period of dietary restriction (rebound), the fact that weight loss by exercise increases as time passes highlights the long-term benefit of exercise. Therefore, exercise as a habit helps to maintain a healthy body weight.

Exercise Brings the Lost Cognitive Functions Back

The second reason for including exercise is that exercise is better than diet at improving cognitive functions and psychological health in overweight and obese people. This is another way to say that exercise is better at bringing the lost cognitive functions and psychological health back. In 2014, Dennis Villareal at Baylor College of Medicine performed the first randomized controlled trial to compare the effect of diet, exercise, and diet plus exercise on cognitive and emotional functioning in obese people (older adults). The subjects on average weighted about 100 kg and possessed a BMI of 37. Subjects were randomly assigned to control, diet, exercise, or diet plus exercise group.

(1) Subjects in the control group received general information about a healthy diet and did not participate in any weight loss or exercise program.

(2) Subjects in the diet group were asked to reduce energy intake by 500-750 kcal/day.

(3) Subjects in the exercise group were directed to maintain a weight-stable diet and participate in three sessions of 90-minute exercise per week. Each exercise session included 15 minutes of flexibility activities, 30 minutes of aerobic exercise, 30 minutes of resistance training, and 15 minutes of balance exercise.

(4) Subjects in the diet plus exercise group participated in both the diet and exercise treatment.

The interventions lasted for a year. A year later, Villareal found that subjects in the diet group and diet plus exercise group lost about 9 kg in body weight, while body weight of those in the exercise group and control group was not changed. This somewhat follows the results of the above Mills 2014 meta-analysis that immediate weight loss by exercise is small. It may also be because in this study the intensity of exercise was relatively low given that the subjects were older people. Research performed in children and adolescents has suggested that time spent in vigorous exercise (such as single tennis, soccer, quick stair climbing) rather than moderate exercise (such as walking, bowling, golf) is associated with lower body fat and higher fitness.

Regarding cognitive and emotional functioning, although the diet group performed better than the control group, the exercise group and diet plus exercise group demonstrated superior performance over the control group and the diet group on almost all the cognitive measures used, including attention, language, and immediate and delayed memory. This finding is understandable given the observation that overweight and obesity are associated with reduced brain volume, and that exercise reverses aging-induced brain loss.

Exercise promotes the brain development of obese people. In a study by Jennifer E. McDowell at the University of Georgia, an 8-month exercise intervention program in overweight and obese children increased white matter integrity in the superior longitudinal fasciculus, a tract that connects frontal and parietal regions. This increased white matter integrity was correlated with improved attention and executive function in these overweight and obese children. Several other randomized controlled trials performed in overweight and obese children and adolescents also suggest that exercise interventions, especially those cognitively challenging such as tennis, benefit the brain and improve executive function and academic achievement.

Exercise Promotes Healthy Diet and Helps to Remove Risk Factors of Obesity

The third reason for including exercise is that exercise improves one's self-regulation capacity, which is a key to losing weight. Healthy dietary habits are a self-regulated behavior, which includes self-monitoring of target behaviors such as logs of food and everyday physical activities. Many factors such as stress, depression, and sleep problems deplete people's capacity for self-regulation. Affected by these factors, people lose control of their eating behaviors.

(1) STRESS: Psychological stress increases the risk of obesity, especially in individuals who use emotional eating as a coping strategy. In the case of acute stress, eating of high-calorie, palatable food may, through improving blood glucose level and activating the brain reward system, boost self-regulation and suppress feelings of stress. However, when this process becomes chronic, weight gain occurs.

(2) DEPRESSION: Depression increases the odds of developing subsequent obesity by 58%. Depressed people show reduced physical activity and may acquire emotional eating habits as a coping strategy. Antidepressant treatments may also have a side effect of increasing weight.

(3) SLEEP PROBLEMS: Poor sleep quality, insufficient sleep (less than 7 hours), oversleep (e.g., > 9 hours for adults), or shiftwork with irregular sleeping patterns increase the risk of obesity. For instance, one study of 2,516 women aged 32-49 years showed that, compared to sleeping for 7 hours of sleep, sleeping for 6, 5, and 2-4 hours per night increased the risk of obesity by 44%, 150%, and 234%, respectively.

Regular exercise, as we have shown, improves self-regulation capacity, buffers stress, prevents and treats depression, and improves sleep quality. This is the third reason that exercise should be combined with diet restriction to lose weight.

###

POSTSCRIPT

Excellence is an art won by training and habituation. We do not act rightly because we have virtue or excellence, but we rather have those because we have acted rightly. We are what we repeatedly do. Excellence, then, is not an act but a habit.

— Aristotle

As we have seen, physical exercise brings positive outcomes in almost every aspect of daily life and across all age spectrums. Physical exercise builds our brain power and therefore boosts mental excellence.

The benefits of exercise are amazing. Yet, exercise alone is not enough. As suggested by many renowned developmental psychologists, our lives are the accumulation of all our life experiences. To what extent we can live a better life depends on how many life strategies we have successfully used. To live a better life, we need more life strategies. That's where "education" comes in. Recall Plato's famous words *"In order for man to succeed in life, God provided him with two means, education and physical activity. Not separately, one for the soul and the other for the body, but for the two together. With these two means, man can attain perfection."* Maximize your education and exercise.

To learn more life strategies, please feel free to sign up for my newsletter at http://brainandlife.net. If you enjoyed this book, please leave a brief review on Amazon or Goodreads. Thanks.

ACKNOWLEDGEMENTS

This book was partially based on my Ph.D. dissertation at Hokkaido University, Sapporo, Japan. I thank my supervisors Professor Kusumi Ichiro and Associate Professor Shin Nakagawa for their guidance. During the composition of this book, many people provided helpful comments. Si Yang, Takaaki Yuzawa, Heather Saxton, Junchao Bian, Yasuhiro Mochizuki, Hans Laubisch, Hermione Bloom, Cate Courtright, Zhengfei Hu, Peng Du, Kanae Shiokawa, and Hua Shi, thank you. I am grateful to my editor Ray Dawn for her professional advice and assistance in polishing this work. All of them have provided insightful ideas — although none is responsible for any errors in this book.

REFERENCES

CHAPTER 1

Two Canadian sports scientists… Leger, L. A., & Lambert, J. (1982). A maximal multistage 20-m shuttle run test to predict VO2 max. *European journal of applied physiology and occupational physiology*, *49*(1), 1-12.

Psychologists Arthur Kramer… Hillman, C. H., Erickson, K. I., & Kramer, A. F. (2008). Be smart, exercise your heart: exercise effects on brain and cognition. *Nature reviews neuroscience*, *9*(1), 58-65.

In a famous study… Duckworth, A. L., & Seligman, M. E. (2005). Self-discipline outdoes IQ in predicting academic performance of adolescents. *Psychological science*, 16(12), 939-944.

is a key to building fitness…Parikh, T., & Stratton, G. (2011). Influence of intensity of physical activity on adiposity and cardiorespiratory fitness in 5–18 year olds. *Sports Medicine*, 41(6), 477-488.

CHAPTER 2

Carol Dweck… http://mindsetonline.com/abouttheauthor/

Parents, teachers, school officers … National Association for Sport and Physical Education and American Heart Association. *2006 shape of the nation report: Status of physical education in the USA*. Reston, VA: National Association for Sport and Physical Education; 2006; Lee, S. M., Burgeson, C. R., Fulton, J. E., & Spain, C. G. (2007). Physical education and physical activity: results from the School Health Policies and Programs Study 2006. *Journal of School Health*, *77*(8), 435-463; Dobson,

N.W. (1999). *Influences on the development of outdoor pursuits in French children's education*. University of Leicester, UK. Dissertation

A 2003 survey… Wilkins, J., Graham, G., Parker, S., Westfall, S., Fraser, R., & Tembo, M. (2003). Time in the arts and physical education and school achievement. *J. Curriculum Studies, 35*(6), 721-734.

In a study of over 300… Tremarche, P. V., Robinson, E. M., & Graham, L. B. (2007). Physical education and its effect on elementary testing results. *Physical Educator, 64*(2), 58.

In another Canadian study… Shephard, R. J. (1996). Habitual physical activity and academic performance. *Nutrition reviews, 54*(4), S32.

Several national health surveys… Dwyer, T., Sallis, J. F., Blizzard, L., Lazarus, R., & Dean, K. (2001). Relation of academic performance to physical activity and fitness in children. *Pediatric Exercise Science, 13*(3), 225-237; Nelson, M. C., & Gordon-Larsen, P. (2006). Physical activity and sedentary behavior patterns are associated with selected adolescent health risk behaviors. *Pediatrics, 117*(4), 1281-1290.

So far, scientists have… Sibley, B. A., & Etnier, J. L. (2003). The relationship between physical activity and cognition in children: a meta-analysis. *Pediatric exercise science, 15*(3), 243-256; Fedewa, A. L., & Ahn, S. (2011). The effects of physical activity and physical fitness on children's achievement and cognitive outcomes: a meta-analysis. *Research quarterly for exercise and sport, 82*(3), 521-535.

A 2008 meta-analysis… Standley, J.M., 2008. Does music instruction help children learn to read? Evidence of a meta-analysis. *Update: Applications of Research in Music Education, 27*(1), pp.17-32.

One study compared… Roberts, C. K., Freed, B., & McCarthy, W. J. (2010). Low aerobic fitness and obesity are associated with lower standardized test scores in children. *The Journal of pediatrics, 156*(5), 711-718.

Genetic research shows… Åberg, M. A., Pedersen, N. L., Torén, K., Svartengren, M., Bäckstrand, B., Johnsson, T.,… & Kuhn, H. G. (2009). Cardiovascular fitness is associated with cognition in young adulthood. *Proceedings of the National Academy of Sciences*, *106*(49), 20906-20911.

Here is the answer... Chang, Y. K., Labban, J. D., Gapin, J. I., & Etnier, J. L. (2012). The effects of acute exercise on cognitive performance: a meta-analysis. *Brain research*, *1453*, 87-101; Lambourne, K., & Tomporowski, P. (2010). The effect of exercise-induced arousal on cognitive task performance: a meta-regression analysis. *Brain research*, *1341*, 12-24; Fedewa, A. L., & Ahn, S. (2011). The effects of physical activity and physical fitness on children's achievement and cognitive outcomes: a meta-analysis. *Research quarterly for exercise and sport*, *82*(3), 521-535; Ballester, R., Huertas, F., Molina, E., & Sanabria, D. (2017). Sport participation and vigilance in children: Influence of different sport expertise. *Journal of Sport and Health Science*; Castelli, D. M., Hillman, C. H., Hirsch, J., Hirsch, A., & Drollette, E. (2011). FIT Kids: Time in target heart zone and cognitive performance. *Preventive Medicine*, *52*, S55-S59; Budde, H., Voelcker-Rehage, C., Pietraßyk-Kendziorra, S., Ribeiro, P., & Tidow, G. (2008). Acute coordinative exercise improves attentional performance in adolescents. *Neuroscience letters*, *441*(2), 219-223; Travlos, A. K. (2010). High intensity physical education classes and cognitive performance in eighth-grade students: An applied study. *International Journal of Sport and Exercise Psychology*, *8*(3), 302-311.

various national or international guidelines... Tremblay, M. S., Warburton, D. E., Janssen, I., Paterson, D. H., Latimer, A. E., Rhodes, R. E.,... & Murumets, K. (2011). New Canadian physical activity guidelines. *Applied Physiology, Nutrition, and Metabolism*, *36*(1), 36-46; U.S. Department of Health and Human Services. 2008 *Physical activity guidelines for Americans*. President's Council on Physical Fitness & Sports Research Digest 9, 1–8 (2008); Who, W. H. O. *Global recommendations on physical activity for health*. Geneva: World Health Organization (2010). doi:10.1080/11026480410034349; Liu, Y. (2017). Promoting physical activity among Chinese youth: No time to wait. *Journal of Sport and Health Science*.

the Committee on... Kohl III, H. W., & Cook, H. D. (Eds.). (2013). *Educating the student body: Taking physical activity and physical education to school.* National Academies Press.

CHAPTER 3

Ishihara made an exciting finding... Ishihara, T., Sugasawa, S., Matsuda, Y., & Mizuno, M. (2017). The beneficial effects of game-based exercise using age-appropriate tennis lessons on the executive functions of 6–12-year-old children. *Neuroscience Letters, 642,* 97-101.

general intelligence... Nisbett, R. E. (2009). *Intelligence and how to get it: Why schools and cultures count.* WW Norton & Company; McCabe, D. P., Roediger III, H. L., McDaniel, M. A., Balota, D. A., & Hambrick, D. Z. (2010). The relationship between working memory capacity and executive functioning: evidence for a common executive attention construct. *Neuropsychology, 24*(2), 222; Conway, A. R., Kane, M. J., & Engle, R. W. (2003). Working memory capacity and its relation to general intelligence. *Trends in cognitive sciences, 7*(12), 547-552.

during the aging process... Troyer, A. K., Leach, L., & Strauss, E. (2006). Aging and response inhibition: Normative data for the Victoria Stroop Test. *Aging, Neuropsychology, and Cognition, 13*(1), 20-35.

Cell phone use while... Redelmeier, D.A. and Tibshirani, R.J., 1997. Association between cellular-telephone calls and motor vehicle collisions. New England Journal of Medicine, 336(7), pp.453-458.

Stressed, depressed, sleep deprived... Qin, S., Hermans, E. J., van Marle, H. J., Luo, J., & Fernández, G. (2009). Acute psychological stress reduces working memory-related activity in the dorsolateral prefrontal cortex. *Biological psychiatry,* 66(1), 25-32; Beers, S. R., & De Bellis, M. D. (2002). Neuropsychological function in children with maltreatment-related posttraumatic stress disorder. *American Journal of Psychiatry, 159*(3), 483-486; Snyder, H. R. (2013). Major depressive disorder is associated with broad impairments on neuropsychological measures of executive function: A meta-analysis and review; Lim, J., & Dinges, D. F. (2010). A meta-analysis of the impact of short-term sleep deprivation on cognitive variables; Moran, T. P. (2016). Anxiety and working memory capacity: A meta-analysis and narrative review;

Eysenck, M. W., Derakshan, N., Santos, R., & Calvo, M. G. (2007). Anxiety and cognitive performance: attentional control theory. *Emotion*, *7*(2), 336.

In a more recent study... Ishihara, T., Sugasawa, S., Matsuda, Y., & Mizuno, M. (in press). Relationship of tennis play to executive function in children and adolescents. *European Journal of Sport Science*

Hillman and Kramer... Hillman, C. H., Pontifex, M. B., Castelli, D. M., Khan, N. A., Raine, L. B., Scudder, M. R.,... & Kamijo, K. (2014). Effects of the FITKids randomized controlled trial on executive control and brain function. *Pediatrics*, *134*(4), e1063-e1071; Scudder, M. R., Drollette, E. S., Szabo-Reed, A. N., Lambourne, K., Fenton, C. I., Donnelly, J. E., & Hillman, C. H. (2016). Tracking the relationship between children's aerobic fitness and cognitive control. *Health Psychology*, *35*(9), 967; Chaddock-Heyman, L., Erickson, K. I., Voss, M., Knecht, A., Pontifex, M. B., Castelli, D.,... & Kramer, A. (2013). The effects of physical activity on functional MRI activation associated with cognitive control in children: a randomized controlled intervention. *Frontiers in human neuroscience*, *7*, 72.

people with higher IQ... Neubauer, A. C., & Fink, A. (2009). Intelligence and neural efficiency. *Neuroscience & Biobehavioral Reviews*, *33*(7), 1004-1023.

CHAPTER 4

using structural MRI... Chaddock, L., Erickson, K. I., Prakash, R. S., Kim, J. S., Voss, M. W., VanPatter, M.,... & Cohen, N. J. (2010). A neuroimaging investigation of the association between aerobic fitness, hippocampal volume, and memory performance in preadolescent children. *Brain research*, *1358*, 172-183.

the Canadian neuroscientist... Squire, L. R. (2009). The legacy of patient HM for neuroscience. Neuron, 61(1), 6-9.

Children with higher aerobic... Herting, M. M., & Nagel, B. J. (2012). Aerobic fitness relates to learning on a virtual Morris Water Task and hippocampal volume in adolescents. *Behavioural brain research*, *233*(2), 517-525.

Smith, P. J., Blumenthal, J. A., Hoffman, B. M., Cooper, H., Strauman, T. A., Welsh-Bohmer, K.,... & Sherwood, A. (2010). Aerobic exercise and neurocognitive performance: a meta-analytic review of randomized controlled trials. *Psychosomatic medicine, 72*(3), 239.

Cotman, C. W., Berchtold, N. C., & Christie, L. A. (2007). Exercise builds brain health: key roles of growth factor cascades and inflammation. *Trends in neurosciences, 30*(9), 464-472.

Szuhany, K. L., Bugatti, M., & Otto, M. W. (2015). A meta-analytic review of the effects of exercise on brain-derived neurotrophic factor. *Journal of psychiatric research, 60*, 56-64.

many experiences... Henson, R. N., Campbell, K. L., Davis, S. W., Taylor, J. R., Emery, T., Erzinclioglu, S., & Kievit, R. A. (2016). Multiple determinants of lifespan memory differences. *Scientific reports, 6*, 32527; Raz, N., Lindenberger, U., Rodrigue, K. M., Kennedy, K. M., Head, D., Williamson, A.,... & Acker, J. D. (2005). Regional brain changes in aging healthy adults: general trends, individual differences and modifiers. *Cerebral cortex, 15*(11), 1676-1689; Gianaros, P. J., Jennings, J. R., Sheu, L. K., Greer, P. J., Kuller, L. H., & Matthews, K. A. (2007). Prospective reports of chronic life stress predict decreased grey matter volume in the hippocampus. *Neuroimage, 35*(2), 795-803; McEwen, B. S. (2006). Protective and damaging effects of stress mediators: central role of the brain. *Dialogues in clinical neuroscience, 8*(4), 367; Opel, N., Redlich, R., Zwanzger, P., Grotegerd, D., Arolt, V., Heindel, W.,... & Dannlowski, U. (2014). Hippocampal atrophy in major depression: a function of childhood maltreatment rather than diagnosis?. *Neuropsychopharmacology, 39*(12), 2723-2731; O'Brien, J. T., Lloyd, A., McKeith, I., Gholkar, A., & Ferrier, N. (2004). A longitudinal study of hippocampal volume, cortisol levels, and cognition in older depressed subjects. *American Journal of Psychiatry, 161*(11), 2081-2090; Erickson, K. I., Colcombe, S. J., Raz, N., Korol, D. L., Scalf, P., Webb, A.,... & Kramer, A. F. (2005). Selective sparing of brain tissue in postmenopausal women receiving hormone replacement therapy. *Neurobiology of aging, 26*(8), 1205-1213; Beresford, T. P., Arciniegas, D. B., Alfers, J., Clapp, L., Martin, B., Du, Y.,... & Davatzikos, C. (2006). Hippocampus volume loss due to chronic heavy drinking. *Alcoholism: Clinical and Experimental Research, 30*(11), 1866-1870.

In a 2011 study... Erickson, K. I., Voss, M. W., Prakash, R. S., Basak, C., Szabo, A., Chaddock, L.,... & Wojcicki, T. R. (2011). Exercise training increases size of hippocampus and improves memory. *Proceedings of the National Academy of Sciences, 108*(7), 3017-3022.

BDNF... Voss, M. W., Vivar, C., Kramer, A. F., & van Praag, H. (2013). Bridging animal and human models of exercise-induced brain plasticity. *Trends in cognitive sciences, 17*(10), 525-544.

neurogenesis... Altman, J., & Das, G. D. (1965). Autoradiographic and histological evidence of postnatal hippocampal neurogenesis in rats. *Journal of Comparative Neurology, 124*(3), 319-335; Gould, E., Tanapat, P., McEwen, B. S., Flügge, G., & Fuchs, E. (1998). Proliferation of granule cell precursors in the dentate gyrus of adult monkeys is diminished by stress. *Proceedings of the National Academy of Sciences, 95*(6), 3168-3171; Eriksson, P. S., Perfilieva, E., Björk-Eriksson, T., Alborn, A. M., Nordborg, C., Peterson, D. A., & Gage, F. H. (1998). Neurogenesis in the adult human hippocampus. *Nature medicine, 4*(11), 1313-1317; Deng, W., Aimone, J. B., & Gage, F. H. (2010). New neurons and new memories: how does adult hippocampal neurogenesis affect learning and memory?. *Nature Reviews Neuroscience, 11*(5), 339-350; Sahay, A., Scobie, K. N., Hill, A. S., O'carroll, C. M., Kheirbek, M. A., Burghardt, N. S.,... & Hen, R. (2011). Increasing adult hippocampal neurogenesis is sufficient to improve pattern separation. *Nature, 472*(7344), 466-470.

Henriette van Praag... Van Praag, H., Christie, B. R., Sejnowski, T. J., & Gage, F. H. (1999). Running enhances neurogenesis, learning, and long-term potentiation in mice. *Proceedings of the National Academy of Sciences, 96*(23), 13427-13431.

a potential solution... Palmer, T. D., Willhoite, A. R., & Gage, F. H. (2000). Vascular niche for adult hippocampal neurogenesis. *Journal of Comparative Neurology, 425*(4), 479-494

Pereira asked middle-aged... Pereira, A. C., Huddleston, D. E., Brickman, A. M., Sosunov, A. A., Hen, R., McKhann, G. M.,... & Small, S. A. (2007).

An in vivo correlate of exercise-induced neurogenesis in the adult dentate gyrus. *Proceedings of the National Academy of Sciences, 104*(13), 5638-5643.

CHAPTER 5

Three decades ago... Thayer, R. E. (1987). Problem perception, optimism, and related states as a function of time of day (diurnal rhythm) and moderate exercise: Two arousal systems in interaction. *Motivation and Emotion, 11*(1), 19-36; Thayer, R. E. (1987). Energy, tiredness, and tension effects of a sugar snack versus moderate exercise. *Journal of personality and social psychology, 52*(1), 119; Thayer, R. E., Peters, D. P., Takahashi, P. J., & Birkhead-Flight, A. M. (1993). Mood and behavior (smoking and sugar snacking) following moderate exercise: A partial test of self-regulation theory. *Personality and Individual Differences, 14*(1), 97-104.

other physical activities are also... Williamson, D., Dewey, A., & Steinberg, H. (2001). Mood change through physical exercise in nine-to ten-year-old children. *Perceptual and Motor Skills, 93*(1), 311-316.

A meta-analysis of... Reed, J., & Ones, D. S. (2006). The effect of acute aerobic exercise on positive activated affect: A meta-analysis. *Psychology of Sport and Exercise, 7*(5), 477-514.

scientists asked people to list... Thayer, R. E., Newman, J. R., & McClain, T. M. (1994). Self-regulation of mood: Strategies for changing a bad mood, raising energy, and reducing tension. *Journal of personality and social psychology, 67*(5), 910.

28.000 people... Taquet, M., Quoidbach, J., de Montjoye, Y. A., Desseilles, M., & Gross, J. J. (2016). Hedonism and the choice of everyday activities. *Proceedings of the National Academy of Sciences*, 201519998.

POSITIVE MOOD BROADENS ATTENTION...POSITIVE MOOD INCREASES CREATIVE THOUGHTS... Fredrickson, B. L. (2013). Positive emotions broaden and build. *Advances in experimental social psychology, 47*(1), 53.

HAPPY STUDENTS LEARN MORE AT SCHOOL... Bryan, T., & Bryan, J. (1991). Positive mood and math performance. *Journal of Learning Disabilities*, *24*(8), 490-494; Bryan, T., Mathur, S., & Sullivan, K. (1996). The impact of positive mood on learning. *Learning Disability Quarterly*, *19*(3), 153-162; Scrimin, S., & Mason, L. (2015). Does mood influence text processing and comprehension? Evidence from an eye-movement study. *British Journal of Educational Psychology*, *85*(3), 387-406.

CHAPTER 6

individuals with high fitness... Boullosa, D. A., Hautala, A. J., & Leicht, A. S. (2014). Introduction to the research topic: the role of physical fitness on cardiovascular responses to stress. *Frontiers in physiology*, *5*; Rodrigues, A. V. S., Martinez, E. C., Duarte, A. F. A., & Ribeiro, L. C. S. (2007). Aerobic fitness and its influence in the mental stress response in army personnel. *Revista Brasileira de Medicina do Esporte*, *13*(2), 113-117; Rauber, S. B., Boullosa, D. A., Carvalho, F. O., de Moraes, J. F., de Sousa, I. R., Simões, H. G., & Campbell, C. S. (2014). Traditional games resulted in post-exercise hypotension and a lower cardiovascular response to the cold pressor test in healthy children. *Frontiers in physiology*, *5*; Bernstein, E. E., & McNally, R. J. (2017). Acute aerobic exercise hastens emotional recovery from a subsequent stressor. *Health Psychology*, *36*(6), 560.

A DOUBLE-EDGED SWORD... Sapolsky, R. M., Krey, L. C., & McEWEN, B. S. (1986). The neuroendocrinology of stress and aging: the glucocorticoid cascade hypothesis. *Endocrine reviews*, *7*(3), 284-301; De Kloet, E. R., Joëls, M., & Holsboer, F. (2005). Stress and the brain: from adaptation to disease. *Nature Reviews Neuroscience*, *6*(6), 463-475; Lupien, S. J., McEwen, B. S., Gunnar, M. R., & Heim, C. (2009). Effects of stress throughout the lifespan on the brain, behaviour and cognition. *Nature Reviews Neuroscience*, *10*(6), 434-445

CHRONIC STRESS DAMAGES THE BRAIN... Karten, Y. J., Olariu, A., & Cameron, H. A. (2005). Stress in early life inhibits neurogenesis in adulthood. *Trends in neurosciences*, *28*(4), 171-172; Luby, J., Belden, A., Botteron, K., Marrus, N., Harms, M. P., Babb, C.,... & Barch, D. (2013). The effects of poverty on childhood brain development: the mediating effect of caregiving and stressful life events. *JAMA pediatrics, 167*(12), 1135-1142; Hair, N. L., Hanson, J. L., Wolfe, B. L., & Pollak, S. D. (2015). Association of child poverty, brain development, and academic achievement. *JAMA pediatrics, 169*(9), 822-829; Butterworth, P., Cherbuin, N., Sachdev, P., & Anstey, K. J. (2012). The association between financial hardship and amygdala and hippocampal volumes: results from the PATH through life project. *Social cognitive and affective neuroscience, 7*(5), 548-556; Driessen, M., Herrmann, J., Stahl, K., Zwaan, M., Meier, S., Hill, A.,... & Petersen, D. (2000). Magnetic resonance imaging volumes of the hippocampus and the amygdala in women with borderline personality disorder and early traumatization. *Archives of general psychiatry, 57*(12), 1115-1122.

Compared to their less-stressed ... Yusoff, M. S. B., Pa, M. N. M., Mey, S. C., Aziz, R. A., & Rahim, A. F. A. (2013). A longitudinal study of relationships between previous academic achievement, emotional intelligence and personality traits with psychological health of medical students during stressful periods. *Education for health, 26*(1), 39; Rothon, C., Head, J., Clark, C., Klineberg, E., Cattell, V., & Stansfeld, S. (2009). The impact of psychological distress on the educational achievement of adolescents at the end of compulsory education. *Social psychiatry and psychiatric epidemiology, 44*(5), 421-427.

children raised in households... Nisbett, R. E. (2009). *Intelligence and how to get it: Why schools and cultures count.* WW Norton & Company

children exposed to maltreatment... Straus, M. A., & Paschall, M. J. (2009). Corporal punishment by mothers and development of children's cognitive ability: A longitudinal study of two nationally representative age cohorts. *Journal of Aggression, Maltreatment & Trauma, 18*(5), 459-483; Koenen, K. C., Moffitt, T. E., Caspi, A., Taylor, A., & Purcell, S. (2003). Domestic violence is associated with environmental suppression of IQ in young children. *Development and psychopathology, 15*(02), 297-311; MacKenzie, M. J., Nicklas, E., Waldfogel, J., & Brooks-Gunn, J. (2012). Corporal punishment and child behavioural and cognitive outcomes through 5 years of age: Evidence from a contemporary urban birth cohort study. *Infant and Child Development, 21*(1), 3-33.

Bullying at school... Konishi, C., Hymel, S., Zumbo, B. D., & Li, Z. (2010). Do school bullying and student—teacher relationships matter for academic achievement? A multilevel analysis. *Canadian Journal of School Psychology*, *25*(1), 19-39; Strøm, I. F., Thoresen, S., Wentzel-Larsen, T., & Dyb, G. (2013). Violence, bullying and academic achievement: A study of 15-year-old adolescents and their school environment. *Child abuse & neglect*, *37*(4), 243-251.

students from classes of teachers... Unterbrink, T., Hack, A., Pfeifer, R., Buhl-Grießhaber, V., Müller, U., Wesche, H.,... & Bauer, J. (2007). Burnout and effort–reward-imbalance in a sample of 949 German teachers. *International archives of occupational and environmental health*, *80*(5), 433-441; Oberle, E., & Schonert-Reichl, K. A. (2016). Stress contagion in the classroom? The link between classroom teacher burnout and morning cortisol in elementary school students. *Social Science & Medicine*, *159*, 30-37; Shen, B., McCaughtry, N., Martin, J., Garn, A., Kulik, N., & Fahlman, M. (2015). The relationship between teacher burnout and student motivation. *British Journal of Educational Psychology*, *85*(4), 519-532; Klusmann, U., Richter, D., & Lüdtke, O. (2016). Teachers' emotional exhaustion is negatively related to students' achievement: Evidence from a large-scale assessment study. *Journal of Educational Psychology*, *108*(8), 1193.

PHYSICALLY ACTIVE INDIVIDUALS EXPERIENCE LESS STRESS... Chen, C. (2016). *The neurobiological basis of the antidepressant-like effect of exercise*; Melville, G. W., Chang, D., Colagiuri, B., Marshall, P. W., & Cheema, B. S. (2012). Fifteen minutes of chair-based yoga postures or guided meditation performed in the office can elicit a relaxation response. *Evidence-Based Complementary and Alternative Medicine*, *2012*; Elliot, C., Lang, C., Brand, S., Holsboer-Trachsler, E., Pühse, U., & Gerber, M. (2015). The relationship between meeting vigorous physical activity recommendations and burnout symptoms among adolescents: an exploratory study with vocational students. *Journal of Sport and Exercise Psychology*, *37*(2), 180-192; Olson, S. M., Odo, N. U., Duran, A. M., Pereira, A. G., & Mandel, J. H. (2014). Burnout and physical activity in Minnesota internal medicine resident physicians. *Journal of graduate medical education*, *6*(4), 669-674; Lindwall, M., Gerber, M., Jonsdottir, I. H., Börjesson, M., & Ahlborg

Jr, G. (2014). The relationships of change in physical activity with change in depression, anxiety, and burnout: A longitudinal study of Swedish healthcare workers. *Health Psychology, 33*(11), 1309; Bretland, R. J., & Thorsteinsson, E. B. (2015). Reducing workplace burnout: The relative benefits of cardiovascular and resistance exercise. *PeerJ, 3*, e891.

CHAPTER 7

In the 1970s… Baumeister, R. F., & Tierney, J. (2011). *Willpower: Rediscovering the greatest human strength*. Penguin.

two Australian psychologists… Oaten, M., & Cheng, K. (2005). Academic examination stress impairs self–control. *Journal of social and clinical psychology, 24*(2), 254-279.

THE FAILURE OF SELF-REGULATION… Hofmann, W., Baumeister, R. F., Förster, G., & Vohs, K. D. (2012). Everyday temptations: an experience sampling study of desire, conflict, and self-control. *Journal of personality and social psychology, 102*(6), 1318; Hofmann, W., Vohs, K. D., & Baumeister, R. F. (2012). What people desire, feel conflicted about, and try to resist in everyday life. *Psychological science, 23*(6), 582-588; Hagger, M. S., Wood, C., Stiff, C., & Chatzisarantis, N. L. (2010). Ego depletion and the strength model of self-control: a meta-analysis; Graham, J. D., & Bray, S. R. (2015). Self-Control Strength Depletion Reduces Self-Efficacy and Impairs Exercise Performance. *Journal of Sport and Exercise Psychology, 37*(5), 477-488

DEPLETED STUDENTS PERFORM… Schmeichel, B. J., Vohs, K. D., & Baumeister, R. F. (2003). Intellectual performance and ego depletion: role of the self in logical reasoning and other information processing. *Journal of personality and social psychology, 85*(1), 33.

WHEN SELF-REGULATION OUTPERFORMS IQ… Mischel, W., Shoda, Y., & Rodriguez, M. L. (1989). Delay of gratification in children. *Science, 244*(4907), 933; Metcalfe, J., & Mischel, W. (1999). A hot/cool-system analysis of delay of gratification: dynamics of willpower. *Psychological review, 106*(1), 3; Duckworth, A. L., & Seligman, M. E. (2005). Self-discipline outdoes IQ in predicting academic performance of adolescents. *Psychological science, 16*(12), 939-944.

SELF-REGULATION AND DEVELOPMENT... Tangney, J. P., Baumeister, R. F., & Boone, A. L. (2004). High self-control predicts good adjustment, less pathology, better grades, and interpersonal success. *Journal of personality*, *72*(2), 271-324; Klapp, A. (2016). The importance of self-regulation and negative emotions for predicting educational outcomes–Evidence from 13-year olds in Swedish compulsory and upper secondary school. *Learning and Individual Differences*, *52*, 29-38; Shiomi, K., Nakata, S., & Joireman, J. A. (1999). Associations of self-regulation with personality traits and self-efficacy in Japanese elementary school children. *Perceptual and motor skills*, *88*(3_suppl), 1169-1172; Birch, L. L., & Fisher, J. O. (1998). Development of eating behaviors among children and adolescents. *Pediatrics*, 101, 539–549; Hankonen, N., Kinnunen, M., Absetz, P., & Jallinoja, P. (2014). Why do people high in self-control eat more healthily? Social cognitions as mediators. *Annals of Behavioral Medicine*, *47*(2), 242-248; Daly, M., Egan, M., Quigley, J., Delaney, L., & Baumeister, R. F. (2016). Childhood self-control predicts smoking throughout life: Evidence from 21,000 cohort study participants. *Health Psychology*, *35*(11), 1254; Quinn, P. D., & Fromme, K. (2010). Self-regulation as a protective factor against risky drinking and sexual behavior. *Psychology of Addictive Behaviors*, *24*(3), 376; Hankonen, N., Kinnunen, M., Absetz, P., & Jallinoja, P. (2014). Why do people high in self-control eat more healthily? Social cognitions as mediators. *Annals of Behavioral Medicine*, *47*(2), 242-248.

STRATEGIES TO BOOST... McNay, E. C., Fries, T. M., & Gold, P. E. (2000). Decreases in rat extracellular hippocampal glucose concentration associated with cognitive demand during a spatial task. *Proceedings of the National Academy of Sciences USA*, 97, 2881-2885; Feldman J, Barshi I: *The Effects of Blood Glucose Levels on Cognitive Performance: a Review of Literature*. Moffett Field, California, NASA Ames Research Center, 2007 (NASA/TM-2007-214555); Tice, D. M., Baumeister, R. F., Shmeuli, D., & Muraven, M. (2007). Restoring the self: Positive affect helps improve self-regulation following ego depletion. *Journal of Experimental Social Psychology*, 43, 379-384; Boksem, M. A., Meijman, T. F., & Lorist, M. M. (2006). Mental fatigue, motivation and action monitoring. *Biological psychology*, *72*(2), 123-132; Muraven, M.,

Baumeister, R. F., & Tice, D. M. (1999). Longitudinal improvement of self-regulation through practice: Building self-control strength through repeated exercise. *The Journal of social psychology, 139*(4), 446-457; Muraven, M. (2010). Building self-control strength: Practicing self-control leads to improved self-control performance. *Journal of experimental social psychology, 46*(2), 465-468.

Exercise promotes self-regulation… Oaten, M., & Cheng, K. (2006). Longitudinal gains in self-regulation from regular physical exercise. *British journal of health psychology, 11*(4), 717-733; Oaten, M., & Cheng, K. (2006). Improved self-control: The benefits of a regular program of academic study. *Basic and Applied Social Psychology, 28*(1), 1-16.

CHAPTER 8

the smartphone game… Grohol, J.M., (2016). Pokemon Go Reportedly Helping People's Mental Health, Depression. https://psychcentral.com/blog/archives/2016/07/11/pokemon-go-reportedly-helping-peoples-mental-health-depression/

DEPRESSION AS LEARNED HELPLESSNESS… Maier, S. F., & Seligman, M. E. (2016). Learned helplessness at fifty: Insights from neuroscience. Psychological review, 123(4), 349; Abramson, L. Y., Seligman, M. E., & Teasdale, J. D. (1978). Learned helplessness in humans: Critique and reformulation. *Journal of abnormal psychology, 87*(1), 49.

two major factors… Hammen, C. (2005). Stress and depression. *Annu. Rev. Clin. Psychol., 1*, 293-319; Abramson, L. Y., Alloy, L. B., Hankin, B. L., Haeffel, G. J., MacCoon, D. G., & Gibb, B. E. (2002). Cognitive vulnerability-stress models of depression in a self-regulatory and psychobiological context; Beck, A. T., & Bredemeier, K. (2016). A unified model of depression: Integrating clinical, cognitive, biological, and evolutionary perspectives. *Clinical Psychological Science, 4*(4), 596-619; Hankin, B. L., Abramson, L. Y., Miller, N., & Haeffel, G. J. (2004). Cognitive vulnerability-stress theories of depression: Examining affective specificity in the prediction of depression versus anxiety in three prospective studies. *Cognitive Therapy and Research, 28*(3), 309-345; Vinkers, C. H., Joëls, M., Milaneschi, Y., Kahn, R. S., Penninx, B. W., &

Boks, M. P. (2014). Stress exposure across the life span cumulatively increases depression risk and is moderated by neuroticism. *Depression and anxiety*, *31*(9), 737-745; Orth, U., Robins, R. W., Meier, L. L., & Conger, R. D. (2016). Refining the vulnerability model of low self-esteem and depression: Disentangling the effects of genuine self-esteem and narcissism. *Journal of Personality and Social Psychology*, *110*(1), 133; Nolen-Hoeksema, S., Girgus, J. S., & Seligman, M. E. (1986). Learned helplessness in children: A longitudinal study of depression, achievement, and explanatory style. *Journal of personality and social psychology*, *51*(2), 435; Van Eck, M., Berkhof, H., Nicolson, N., & Sulon, J. (1996). The effects of perceived stress, traits, mood states, and stressful daily events on salivary cortisol. *Psychosomatic medicine*, *58*(5), 447-458; Gilbertson, M. W., Shenton, M. E., Ciszewski, A., Kasai, K., Lasko, N. B., Orr, S. P., & Pitman, R. K. (2002). Smaller hippocampal volume predicts pathologic vulnerability to psychological trauma. *Nature neuroscience*, *5*(11), 1242-1247.

vulnerabilities are often caused… Henry, C., Kabbaj, M., Simon, H., Moal, M., & Maccari, S. (1994). Prenatal stress increases the hypothalamo-pituitary-adrenal axis response in young and adult rats. *Journal of neuroendocrinology*, *6*(3), 341-345; Koehl, M., Darnaudéry, M., Dulluc, J., Van Reeth, O., Moal, M. L., & Maccari, S. (1999). Prenatal stress alters circadian activity of hypothalamo–pituitary–adrenal axis and hippocampal corticosteroid receptors in adult rats of both gender. *Developmental Neurobiology*, *40*(3), 302-315; Kendler, K. S., & Karkowski-Shuman, L. (1997). Stressful life events and genetic liability to major depression: genetic control of exposure to the environment?. *Psychological medicine*, *27*(03), 539-547; Clauss, J. A., Avery, S. N., & Blackford, J. U. (2015). The nature of individual differences in inhibited temperament and risk for psychiatric disease: A review and meta-analysis. *Progress in neurobiology*, *127*, 23-45.

Depression is not simply… American Psychiatric Association. (2014). *The Fifth Edition of the Diagnostic and Statistical Manual of Mental Disorders (DSM-5)*. Washington DC, APA.

psychologist Hannah Snyder... Snyder, H. R. (2013). Major depressive disorder is associated with broad impairments on neuropsychological measures of executive function: A meta-analysis and review.

but difficult to treat clinically... Marcus, M., Yasamy, M. T., van Ommeren, M. & Chisholdepressionepression, a global public health concern. WHO Department of Mental Health and Substance Abuse 1–8 (2012). http://www.who.int/mental_health/management/depression/who_paper_ depression_wfmh_2012.pdf; Kessler, R. C., & Bromet, E. J. (2013). The epidemiology of depression across cultures. *Annual review of public health*, *34*, 119-138; WPRO | Fact sheet on adolescent health; Rush, A. J., Trivedi, M. H., Wisniewski, S. R., Nierenberg, A. A., Stewart, J. W., Warden, D.,... & McGrath, P. J. (2006). Acute and longer-term outcomes in depressed outpatients requiring one or several treatment steps: a STAR* D report. *American Journal of Psychiatry*, *163*(11), 1905-1917; Murray, C. J., & Lopez, A. D. (1996). Evidence-based health policy--lessons from the Global Burden of Disease Study. *Science*, *274*(5288), 740; Murray, C. J., Lopez, A. D., & World Health Organization. (1996). The global burden of disease: a comprehensive assessment of mortality and disability from diseases, injuries, and risk factors in 1990 and projected to 2020: summary; WHO | Estimates for 2000–2012.

STUDENTS WITH HIGH DEPRESSIVE... Brière, F. N., Janosz, M., Fallu, J. S., & Morizot, J. (2015). Adolescent trajectories of depressive symptoms: codevelopment of behavioral and academic problems. *Journal of Adolescent Health*, *57*(3), 313-319; Hishinuma, E. S., Chang, J. Y., McArdle, J. J., & Hamagami, F. (2012). Potential causal relationship between depressive symptoms and academic achievement in the Hawaiian high schools health survey using contemporary longitudinal latent variable change models. *Developmental psychology*, *48*(5), 1327; Repetto, P. B., Caldwell, C. H., & Zimmerman, M. A. (2004). Trajectories of depressive symptoms among high risk African-American adolescents. *Journal of adolescent health*, *35*(6), 468-477; Verboom, C. E., Sijtsema, J. J., Verhulst, F. C., Penninx, B. W., & Ormel, J. (2014). Longitudinal associations between depressive problems, academic performance, and social functioning in adolescent boys and girls. *Developmental psychology*, *50*(1), 247; Chow, C. M., Tan, C. C., &

Buhrmester, D. (2015). Interdependence of depressive symptoms, school involvement, and academic performance between adolescent friends: A dyadic analysis. *British Journal of Educational Psychology, 85*(3), 316-331.

A 2002 WHO survey...

http://www.euro.who.int/__data/assets/pdf_file/0006/119571/E67880.pdf

AS LITTLE AS 10-29 MINUTES... Liu, M., Wu, L., & Ming, Q. (2015). How does physical activity intervention improve self-esteem and self-concept in children and adolescents? Evidence from a meta-analysis. *PloS one, 10*(8), e0134804; Park, S. H., Han, K. S., & Kang, C. B. (2014). Effects of exercise programs on depressive symptoms, quality of life, and self-esteem in older people: A systematic review of randomized controlled trials. *Applied Nursing Research, 27*(4), 219-226; Salmon, P. (2001). Effects of physical exercise on anxiety, depression, and sensitivity to stress: a unifying theory. *Clinical psychology review, 21*(1), 33-61; Teychenne, M., Ball, K., & Salmon, J. (2008). Physical activity and likelihood of depression in adults: a review. *Preventive medicine, 46*(5), 397-411; Mammen, G., & Faulkner, G. (2013). Physical activity and the prevention of depression: a systematic review of prospective studies. *American journal of preventive medicine, 45*(5), 649-657.

EXERCISE AS A POTENT THERAPY... Pinquart, M., Duberstein, P. R., & Lyness, J. M. (2007). Effects of psychotherapy and other behavioral interventions on clinically depressed older adults: a meta-analysis. *Aging & mental health, 11*(6), 645-657; Cooney, G., Dwan, K., & Mead, G. (2014). Exercise for depression. *Jama, 311*(23), 2432-2433; Mata, J., Thompson, R. J., Jaeggi, S. M., Buschkuehl, M., Jonides, J., & Gotlib, I. H. (2012). Walk on the bright side: physical activity and affect in major depressive disorder. *Journal of abnormal psychology, 121*(2), 297.

CHAPTER 9

Randy Gardner... Randall, D. K. (2012). Dreamland: Adventures in the strange science of sleep. WW Norton & Company.

a meta-analysis of 147... Lim, J., & Dinges, D. F. (2010). A meta-analysis of the impact of short-term sleep deprivation on cognitive variables.

nurses get on average... Caldwell, J. A., Mallis, M. M., Caldwell, J. L., Paul, M. A., Miller, J. C., & Neri, D. F. (2009). Fatigue countermeasures in aviation. *Aviation, space, and environmental medicine, 80*(1), 29-59

are equally affected... Linde, L., & Bergströme, M. (1992). The effect of one night without sleep on problem-solving and immediate recall. *Psychological research, 54*(2), 127-136; Polzella, D. J. (1975). Effects of sleep deprivation on short-term recognition memory. *Journal of Experimental Psychology: Human Learning and Memory, 1*(2), 194; Jewett, M. E., Dijk, D. J., Kronauer, R. E., & Dinges, D. F. (1999). Dose-response relationship between sleep duration and human psychomotor vigilance and subjective alertness. *Sleep: Journal of Sleep Research & Sleep Medicine.*

SLEEP IS NECESSARY FOR MEMORY... Wilson, M. A., & McNaughton, B. L. (1994). Reactivation of hippocampal ensemble memories during sleep. *Science, 265*(5172), 676-679; Inostroza, M., & Born, J. (2013). Sleep for preserving and transforming episodic memory. *Annual review of neuroscience, 36*, 79-102; Walker, M. P., & Stickgold, R. (2006). Sleep, memory, and plasticity. *Annu. Rev. Psychol., 57*, 139-166; Wang, S. H., & Morris, R. G. (2010). Hippocampal-neocortical interactions in memory formation, consolidation, and reconsolidation. *Annual review of psychology, 61*, 49-79; Diekelmann, S., & Born, J. (2010). The memory function of sleep. *Nature Reviews Neuroscience, 11*(2), 114-126; Stickgold, R., & Walker, M. P. (2013). Sleep-dependent memory triage: evolving generalization through selective processing. *Nature neuroscience, 16*(2), 139-145.

POOR SLEEP INDUCES BAD MOODS... Supartini, A., Honda, T., Basri, N. A., Haeuchi, Y., Chen, S., Ichimiya, A., & Kumagai, S. (2016). The Impact of Sleep Timing, Sleep Duration, and Sleep Quality on Depressive Symptoms and Suicidal Ideation amongst Japanese Freshmen: The EQUSITE Study. *Sleep disorders, 2016*; Hyde, A. L., Conroy, D. E., Pincus, A. L., & Ram, N. (2011). Unpacking the feel-good effect of free-time physical activity: Between-and within-person associations with pleasant–activated feeling states. *Journal of Sport and Exercise Psychology, 33*(6), 884-902; Roberts, R. E., Roberts, C. R., & Duong, H.

T. (2008). Chronic insomnia and its negative consequences for health and functioning of adolescents: a 12-month prospective study. *Journal of Adolescent Health*, *42*(3), 294-302; Szklo-Coxe, M., Young, T., Peppard, P. E., Finn, L. A., & Benca, R. M. (2010). Prospective associations of insomnia markers and symptoms with depression. *American journal of epidemiology*, kwp454; Baglioni, C., Battagliese, G., Feige, B., Spiegelhalder, K., Nissen, C., Voderholzer, U.,... & Riemann, D. (2011). Insomnia as a predictor of depression: a meta-analytic evaluation of longitudinal epidemiological studies. *Journal of affective disorders*, *135*(1), 10-19.

STUDENTS WITH POOR... Wolfson, A. R., & Carskadon, M. A. (1998). Sleep schedules and daytime functioning in adolescents. *Child development*, *69*(4), 875-887; Short, M. A., Gradisar, M., Lack, L. C., & Wright, H. R. (2013). The impact of sleep on adolescent depressed mood, alertness and academic performance. *Journal of adolescence*, *36*(6), 1025-1033; Howell, A. J., Jahrig, J. C., & Powell, R. A. (2004). Sleep quality, sleep propensity and academic performance. *Perceptual and motor skills*, *99*(2), 525-535; Dewald, J. F., Meijer, A. M., Oort, F. J., Kerkhof, G. A., & Bögels, S. M. (2010). The influence of sleep quality, sleep duration and sleepiness on school performance in children and adolescents: a meta-analytic review. *Sleep medicine reviews*, *14*(3), 179-189.

A 2002 WHO...

http://www.euro.who.int/__data/assets/pdf_file/0006/119571/E67880.pdf

light-emitting electronic... Chang, A. M., Aeschbach, D., Duffy, J. F., & Czeisler, C. A. (2015). Evening use of light-emitting eReaders negatively affects sleep, circadian timing, and next-morning alertness. *Proceedings of the National Academy of Sciences*, *112*(4), 1232-1237; Grover, K., Pecor, K., Malkowski, M., Kang, L., Machado, S., Lulla, R.,... & Ming, X. (2016). Effects of instant messaging on school performance in adolescents. *Journal of child neurology*, *31*(7), 850-857.

adults need about... Hirshkowitz, M., Whiton, K., Albert, S. M., Alessi, C., Bruni, O., DonCarlos, L.,... & Neubauer, D. N. (2015). National Sleep

Foundation's sleep time duration recommendations: methodology and results summary. *Sleep Health*, *1*(1), 40-43.

strategies that help to optimize... Dautovich, N.D., Shoji, K.D. and McCrae, C.S., (2013). Variety is the Spice of Life: A Microlongitudinal Study Examining Age Differences in Intraindividual Variability in Daily Activities in Relation to Sleep Outcomes. *The Journals of Gerontology Series B: Psychological Sciences and Social Sciences*, p.gbt120; Caldwell, J. A., Mallis, M. M., Caldwell, J. L., Paul, M. A., Miller, J. C., & Neri, D. F. (2009). Fatigue countermeasures in aviation. *Aviation, space, and environmental medicine*, *80*(1), 29-59; Myllymäki, T., Kyröläinen, H., Savolainen, K., Hokka, L., Jakonen, R., Juuti, T.,... & Rusko, H. (2011). Effects of vigorous late-night exercise on sleep quality and cardiac autonomic activity. *Journal of sleep research*, *20*(1pt2), 146-153; Buman, M. P., Kline, C. E., Youngstedt, S. D., Phillips, B., De Mello, M. T., & Hirshkowitz, M. (2015). Sitting and television viewing: novel risk factors for sleep disturbance and apnea risk? Results from the 2013 National Sleep Foundation Sleep in America Poll. *CHEST Journal*, *147*(3), 728-734.

REGULAR EXERCISE MAKES... Kredlow, M. A., Capozzoli, M. C., Hearon, B. A., Calkins, A. W., & Otto, M. W. (2015). The effects of physical activity on sleep: a meta-analytic review. *Journal of behavioral medicine*, *38*(3), 427-449; Lang, C., Kalak, N., Brand, S., Holsboer-Trachsler, E., Pühse, U., & Gerber, M. (2016). The relationship between physical activity and sleep from mid adolescence to early adulthood. A systematic review of methodological approaches and meta-analysis. *Sleep medicine reviews*, *28*, 32-45; Yang, P. Y., Ho, K. H., Chen, H. C., & Chien, M. Y. (2012). Exercise training improves sleep quality in middle-aged and older adults with sleep problems: a systematic review. *Journal of physiotherapy*, *58*(3), 157-163; Du, S., Dong, J., Zhang, H., Jin, S., Xu, G., Liu, Z.,... & Sun, Z. (2015). Taichi exercise for self-rated sleep quality in older people: A systematic review and meta-analysis. *International journal of nursing studies*, *52*(1), 368-379; de Vries, J. D., van Hooff, M. L., Geurts, S. A., & Kompier, M. A. (2016). Exercise as an intervention to reduce study-related fatigue among university students: A two-arm parallel randomized controlled trial. *PloS one*, *11*(3), e0152137.

CHAPTER 10

Mehdi Kargarfard… Kargarfard, M., Kelishadi, R., Ziaee, V., Ardalan, G., Halabchi, F., Mazaheri, R.,... & Hayatbakhsh, M. R. (2012). The impact of an after-school physical activity program on health-related fitness of mother/daughter pairs: CASPIAN study. *Preventive medicine, 54*(3), 219-223.

ENRICHED ENVIRONMENT…Van Praag, H., Kempermann, G., & Gage, F. H. (2000). Neural consequences of enviromental enrichment. *Nature Reviews Neuroscience, 1*(3), 191-198; Nithianantharajah, J., & Hannan, A. J. (2006). Enriched environments, experience-dependent plasticity and disorders of the nervous system. *Nature Reviews Neuroscience, 7*(9), 697-709; Simpson, J., & Kelly, J. P. (2011). The impact of environmental enrichment in laboratory rats—behavioural and neurochemical aspects. *Behavioural brain research, 222*(1), 246-264; Hirase, H., & Shinohara, Y. (2014). Transformation of cortical and hippocampal neural circuit by environmental enrichment. *Neuroscience, 280,* 282-298; Yang, J., Hou, C., Ma, N., Liu, J., Zhang, Y., Zhou, J.,... & Li, L. (2007). Enriched environment treatment restores impaired hippocampal synaptic plasticity and cognitive deficits induced by prenatal chronic stress. *Neurobiology of learning and memory, 87*(2), 257-263; Cui, M., Yang, Y., Yang, J., Zhang, J., Han, H., Ma, W.,... & Cao, J. (2006). Enriched environment experience overcomes the memory deficits and depressive-like behavior induced by early life stress. *Neuroscience letters, 404*(1), 208-212.

FAMILIES AT HIGH SOCIAL ECONOMIC… Nisbett, R. E. (2009). *Intelligence and how to get it: Why schools and cultures count.* WW Norton & Company; Duncan, S. C., Strycker, L. A., & Chaumeton, N. R. (2015). Personal, family, and peer correlates of general and sport physical activity among African American, Latino, and White girls. *Journal of health disparities research and practice*, 8(2), 12; Morrissey, J. L., Janz, K. F., Letuchy, E. M., Francis, S. L., & Levy, S. M. (2015). The effect of family and friend support on physical activity through adolescence: a longitudinal study. *International Journal of Behavioral Nutrition and Physical Activity*, 12(1), 103.

PSYCHOLOGICALLY HEALTHY PARENTS... Grant, K. E., Compas, B. E., Thurm, A. E., McMahon, S. D., Gipson, P. Y., Campbell, A. J.,... & Westerholm, R. I. (2006). Stressors and child and adolescent psychopathology: Evidence of moderating and mediating effects. *Clinical psychology review*, *26*(3), 257-283; Bridgett, D. J., Burt, N. M., Edwards, E. S., & Deater-Deckard, K. (2015). Intergenerational transmission of self-regulation: A multidisciplinary review and integrative conceptual framework. *Psychological bulletin*, *141*(3), 602; Murray, L., Lau, P. Y., Arteche, A., Creswell, C., Russ, S., Zoppa, L. D.,... & Cooper, P. (2012). Parenting by anxious mothers: effects of disorder subtype, context and child characteristics. *Journal of Child Psychology and Psychiatry*, *53*(2), 188-196; Morris, A. S., Silk, J. S., Steinberg, L., Myers, S. S., & Robinson, L. R. (2007). The role of the family context in the development of emotion regulation. *Social development*, *16*(2), 361-388; Whipple, E. E., & Webster-Stratton, C. (1991). The role of parental stress in physically abusive families. *Child abuse & neglect*, *15*(3), 279-291; Jester, J. M., Nigg, J. T., Puttler, L. I., Long, J. C., Fitzgerald, H. E., & Zucker, R. A. (2009). Intergenerational transmission of neuropsychological executive functioning. *Brain and cognition*, *70*(1), 145-153; Cuevas, K., Deater-Deckard, K., Kim-Spoon, J., Wang, Z., Morasch, K. C., & Bell, M. A. (2014). A longitudinal intergenerational analysis of executive functions during childhood. *British Journal of Developmental Psychology*, 32, 50–64; Deater-Deckard, K., Sewell, M. D., Petrill, S. A., & Thompson, L. A. (2010). Maternal working memory and reactive negativity in parenting. *Psychological Science*, 21, 75–79; Cuevas, K., Deater-Deckard, K., Kim-Spoon, J., Watson, A. J., Morasch, K. C., & Bell, M. A. (2014). What's mom got to do with it? Contributions of maternal executive function and caregiving to the development of executive function across early childhood. *Developmental Science, 17,* 224–238; Deater-Deckard, K., Wang, Z., Chen, N., & Bell, M. A. (2012). Maternal executive function, harsh parenting, and child conduct problems. *Journal of Child Psychology and Psychiatry, 53,* 1084–1091; Bridgett, D. J., Gartstein, M. A., Putnam, S. P., Lance, K. O., Iddins, E., Waits, R.,. .. Lee, L. (2011). Emerging effortful control in toddlerhood: The role of infant orienting/regulation, maternal effortful control, and maternal time spent in caregiving activities. *Infant Behavior and Development, 34,* 189–199; Buckholdt, K. E., Parra, G. R., & Jobe-Shields, L. (2013). Intergenerational transmission of emotion dysregulation through parental invalidation of emotions: Implications for adolescent internalizing and externalizing behaviors. *Journal of Child and Family Studies, 23,* 324–332; Valiente, C., Lemery-Chalfant, K., & Reiser, M. (2007). Pathways to problem behaviors: Chaotic homes, parent and child effortful control, and parenting. *Social Development, 16,* 249–267

household chaos… Evans, G. W., Ricciuti, H. N., Hope, S., Schoon, I., Bradley, R. H., Corwyn, R. F., & Hazan, C. (2010). Crowding and cognitive development the mediating role of maternal responsiveness among 36-month-old children. *Environment and Behavior, 42*(1), 135-148; Martin, A., Razza, R., & Brooks-Gunn, J. (2012). Specifying the links between household chaos and preschool children's development. *Early Child Development and Care, 182,* 1247–1263.

peers with non-depressed mothers… Hay, D. F., Pawlby, S., Waters, C. S., & Sharp, D. (2008). Antepartum and postpartum exposure to maternal depression: different effects on different adolescent outcomes. *Journal of Child Psychology and Psychiatry, 49*(10), 1079-1088; Murray, L., Arteche, A., Fearon, P., Halligan, S., Croudace, T., & Cooper, P. (2010). The effects of maternal postnatal depression and child sex on academic performance at age 16 years: a developmental approach. *Journal of Child Psychology and Psychiatry, 51*(10), 1150-1159; Murray, L., Arteche, A., Fearon, P., Halligan, S., Goodyer, I., & Cooper, P. (2011). Maternal postnatal depression and the development of depression in offspring up to 16 years of age. *Journal of the American Academy of Child & Adolescent Psychiatry, 50*(5), 460-470.

EXERCISING AS A FAMILY… Carson, J. W., Carson, K. M., Gil, K. M., & Baucom, D. H. (2004). Mindfulness-based relationship enhancement. *Behavior therapy, 35*(3), 471-494; Ruiz, R., Gesell, S. B., Buchowski, M. S., Lambert, W., & Barkin, S. L. (2011). The relationship between Hispanic parents and their preschool-aged children's physical activity. *Pediatrics,* 127(5), 888-895; Karppanen, A. K., Ahonen, S. M., Tammelin, T., Vanhala, M., & Korpelainen, R. (2012). Physical activity and fitness in 8-year-old overweight and normal weight children and their parents. *International journal of circumpolar health,* 71; Duncan, S. C., Strycker, L. A., & Chaumeton, N. R. (2015). Personal, family, and peer correlates of general and sport physical activity among African American, Latino, and White girls. *Journal of health disparities research and practice*, 8(2), 12; Morrissey, J. L., Janz, K. F., Letuchy, E. M., Francis, S. L., & Levy, S. M. (2015). The effect of family and friend support on physical activity through adolescence: a longitudinal study. *International Journal of Behavioral Nutrition and Physical Activity*, 12(1), 103.

CHAPTER 11

Take japan for example…

http://www.mext.go.jp/en/publication/whitepaper/title03/detail03/sdetail03/sdetail03/1372942.htm

THE CONCEPT OF SUCCESSFUL AGING… Neugarten, B. L., Havighurst, R. J., & Tobin, S. S. (1961). The measurement of life satisfaction. *Journal of gerontology*; Rowe, J. W., & Kahn, R. L. (1987). Human aging: usual and successful. Science, 237, 143-150; Ouwehand, C., de Ridder, D. T., & Bensing, J. M. (2007). A review of successful aging models: Proposing proactive coping as an important additional strategy. *Clinical psychology review*, 27(8), 873-884; Depp, C., Vahia, I. V., & Jeste, D. (2010). Successful aging: focus on cognitive and emotional health. *Annual Review of Clinical Psychology*, 6, 527-550.

Longitudinal studies have… Leal, S. L., & Yassa, M. A. (2015). Neurocognitive aging and the hippocampus across species. *Trends in neurosciences*, 38(12), 800-812; Raz, N., Rodrigue, K. M., Head, D., Kennedy, K. M., & Acker, J. D. (2004). Differential aging of the medial temporal lobe a study of a five-year change. *Neurology*, 62(3), 433-438; Raz, N., Lindenberger, U., Rodrigue, K. M., Kennedy, K. M., Head, D., Williamson, A.,… & Acker, J. D. (2005). Regional brain changes in aging healthy adults: general trends, individual differences and modifiers. *Cerebral cortex*, 15(11), 1676-1689; Mungas, D., Harvey, D., Reed, B. R., Jagust, W. J., DeCarli, C., Beckett, L.,… & Chui, H. C. (2005). Longitudinal volumetric MRI change and rate of cognitive decline. *Neurology*, 65(4), 565-571; Jack, C. R., Petersen, R. C., Xu, Y., O'Brien, P. C., Smith, G. E., Ivnik, R. J.,… & Kokmen, E. (1998). Rate of medial temporal lobe atrophy in typical aging and Alzheimer's disease. *Neurology*, 51(4), 993-999; Nyberg, L., Lövdén, M., Riklund, K.,

Lindenberger, U., & Bäckman, L. (2012). Memory aging and brain maintenance. *Trends in cognitive sciences*, 16(5), 292-305.

In 2015, Stephen Anton... Anton, S. D., Woods, A. J., Ashizawa, T., Barb, D., Buford, T. W., Carter, C. S.,... & Dotson, V. (2015). Successful aging: Advancing the science of physical independence in older adults. *Ageing research reviews*, *24*, 304-327.

many social and emotional factors... Vemuri, P., Lesnick, T. G., Przybelski, S. A., Machulda, M., Knopman, D. S., Mielke, M. M.,... & Jack, C. R. (2014). Association of lifetime intellectual enrichment with cognitive decline in the older population. *JAMA neurology*, 71(8), 1017-1024; Plaks, J. E., & Chasteen, A. L. (2013). Entity versus incremental theories predict older adults' memory performance. *Psychology and aging*, 28(4), 948; Hertzog, C., Kramer, A. F., Wilson, R. S., & Lindenberger, U. (2008). Enrichment effects on adult cognitive development can the functional capacity of older adults be preserved and enhanced?. *Psychological science in the public interest*, 9(1), 1-65; Westerhof, G. J., Miche, M., Brothers, A. F., Barrett, A. E., Diehl, M., Montepare, J. M.,... & Wurm, S. (2014). The influence of subjective aging on health and longevity: A meta-analysis of longitudinal data. *Psychology and aging*, 29(4), 793; Robertson, D. A., King-Kallimanis, B. L., & Kenny, R. A. (2016). Negative perceptions of aging predict longitudinal decline in cognitive function. *Psychology and aging*, 31(1), 71; Rickenbach, E. H., Almeida, D. M., Seeman, T. E., & Lachman, M. E. (2014). Daily stress magnifies the association between cognitive decline and everyday memory problems: An integration of longitudinal and diary methods. *Psychology and aging*, 29(4), 852; Albanese, E., Matthews, K. A., Zhang, J., Jacobs, D. R., Whitmer, R. A., Wadley, V. G.,... & Launer, L. J. (2016). Hostile attitudes and effortful coping in young adulthood predict cognition 25 years later. *Neurology*, 86(13), 1227-1234; Wilson, R. S., Krueger, K. R., Arnold, S. E., Schneider, J. A., Kelly, J. F., Barnes, L. L., et al. (2007). Loneliness and risk of Alzheimer disease. *Arch. Gen. Psychiatry* 64, 234–240; Cacioppo, S., Capitanio, J. P., and Cacioppo, J. T. (2014). Toward a neurology of loneliness. *Psychol. Bull.* 140, 1464–1504; Tetzner, J., & Schuth, M. (2016). Anxiety in late adulthood: Associations with gender, education, and physical and cognitive functioning. *Psychology and aging*, *31*(5), 532.

Poor sleep... Scullin, M. K., & Bliwise, D. L. (2015). Sleep, Cognition, and Normal Aging Integrating a Half Century of Multidisciplinary Research. *Perspectives on Psychological Science*, 10(1), 97-137; Blackwell, T., Yaffe, K., Ancoli-Israel, S., Redline, S., Ensrud, K. E., Stefanick, M. L.,... & Osteoporotic Fractures in Men (MrOS) Study Group. (2011). Association of sleep characteristics and cognition in older community-dwelling men: the MrOS sleep study. *Sleep*, *34*(10), 1347; Lim, A. S., Kowgier, M., Yu, L., Buchman, A. S., & Bennett, D. A. (2013). Sleep fragmentation and the risk of incident Alzheimer's disease and cognitive decline in older persons. *Sleep*, *36*(7), 1027; Tworoger, S. S., Lee, S., Schernhammer, E. S., & Grodstein, F. (2006). The association of self-reported sleep duration, difficulty sleeping, and snoring with cognitive function in older women. *Alzheimer Disease & Associated Disorders*, *20*(1), 41-48; Yaffe, K., Laffan, A. M., Harrison, S. L., Redline, S., Spira, A. P., Ensrud, K. E.,... & Stone, K. L. (2011). Sleep-disordered breathing, hypoxia, and risk of mild cognitive impairment and dementia in older women. *Jama*, *306*(6), 613-619.

a vascular disease... Dickstein, D. L., Walsh, J., Brautigam, H., Stockton, S. D., Gandy, S., & Hof, P. R. (2010). Role of vascular risk factors and vascular dysfunction in Alzheimer's disease. *Mount Sinai Journal of Medicine: A Journal of Translational and Personalized Medicine*, *77*(1), 82-102.

psychologists Stanley Colcombe... Colcombe, S., & Kramer, A. F. (2003). Fitness effects on the cognitive function of older adults: a meta-analytic study. *Psychological science*, *14*(2), 125-130; Fleg, J. L. (2012). Aerobic exercise in the elderly: a key to successful aging. *Discovery medicine*, *13*(70), 223-228.

ENRICHED ENVIRONMENT FOR THE ELDERLY... Lenehan, M. E., Summers, M. J., Saunders, N. L., Summers, J. J., Ward, D. D., Ritchie, K., & Vickers, J. C. (2015). Sending Your Grandparents to University Increases Cognitive Reserve: The Tasmanian Healthy Brain Project; Noice, H., Noice, T., & Staines, G. (2004). A short-term intervention to enhance cognitive and affective functioning in older adults. *Journal of aging and health*, *16*(4), 562-585; Antoniou, M., Gunasekera, G. M., & Wong, P. C. (2013). Foreign language training as cognitive therapy for age-related cognitive decline: A hypothesis for future research. *Neuroscience & Biobehavioral Reviews*, *37*(10), 2689-2698; Wilson, R. S., Boyle, P. A., Yang, J., James, B. D., & Bennett, D. A. (2015). Early life instruction in foreign language and music and incidence of mild cognitive impairment. *Neuropsychology*, *29*(2), 292; Hanna-Pladdy, B., and MacKay, A. (2011). The relation between instrumental musical activity and cognitive aging. *Neuropsychology* 25, 378; Hughes, T. F., Chang, C. C. H., Vander Bilt, J., & Ganguli, M. (2010). Engagement in reading and hobbies and risk of incident dementia: the MoVIES project. *American Journal of Alzheimer's Disease & Other Dementias®*, *25*(5), 432-438; Pillai, J. A., Hall, C. B., Dickson, D. W., Buschke, H., Lipton, R. B., & Verghese, J. (2011). Association of crossword puzzle participation with memory decline in persons who develop dementia. *Journal of the International Neuropsychological Society*, *17*(06), 1006-1013; Jenkinson, C. E., Dickens, A. P., Jones, K., Thompson-Coon, J., Taylor, R. S., Rogers, M.,... & Richards, S. H. (2013). Is volunteering a public health intervention? A systematic review and meta-analysis of the health and survival of volunteers. *BMC public health*, *13*(1), 773; Okun, M. A., Yeung, E. W., & Brown, S. (2013). Volunteering by older adults and risk of mortality: A meta-analysis. *Psychology and Aging*, 28(2), 564.

CHAPTER 12

Canadian scientist Tauseef Khan... Khan, T. A., & Sievenpiper, J. L. (2016). Controversies about sugars: results from systematic reviews and meta-analyses on obesity, cardiometabolic disease and diabetes. *European Journal of Nutrition*, 1-19.

According   to   WHO...
http://www.who.int/mediacentre/factsheets/fs311/en/

Because of the smaller brain ... Ronan, L., Alexander-Bloch, A. F., Wagstyl, K., Farooqi, S., Brayne, C., Tyler, L. K., & Fletcher, P. C. (2016). Obesity associated with increased brain age from midlife. *Neurobiology of Aging*, 47, 63-70; Gustafson, D., Lissner, L., Bengtsson, C., Björkelund, C., & Skoog, I. (2004). A 24-year follow-up of body mass index and cerebral atrophy. *Neurology*, 63(10), 1876-1881; Gunstad, J., Paul, R. H., Cohen, R. A., Tate, D. F., Spitznagel, M. B., Grieve, S., & Gordon, E.

(2008). Relationship between body mass index and brain volume in healthy adults. *International Journal of Neuroscience*, 118(11), 1582-1593; Gunstad, J., Paul, R. H., Cohen, R. A., Tate, D. F., Spitznagel, M. B., & Gordon, E. (2007). Elevated body mass index is associated with executive dysfunction in otherwise healthy adults. *Comprehensive psychiatry*, 48(1), 57-61; BROAD COGNITIVE AND EMOTIONAL DEFICITS... Barkin, S. L. (2013). The relationship between executive function and obesity in children and adolescents: a systematic literature review. *Journal of obesity*, 2013; Cournot, M. C. M. J., Marquie, J. C., Ansiau, D., Martinaud, C., Fonds, H., Ferrieres, J., & Ruidavets, J. B. (2006). Relation between body mass index and cognitive function in healthy middle-aged men and women. *Neurology*, 67(7), 1208-1214; Lavagnino, L., Arnone, D., Cao, B., Soares, J. C., & Selvaraj, S. (2016). Inhibitory control in obesity and binge eating disorder: A systematic review and meta-analysis of neurocognitive and neuroimaging studies. *Neuroscience & Biobehavioral Reviews*, 68, 714-726.

Sports scientist... Kamijo, K., Khan, N. A., Pontifex, M. B., Scudder, M. R., Drollette, E. S., Raine, L. B.,... & Hillman, C. H. (2012). The relation of adiposity to cognitive control and scholastic achievement in preadolescent children. *Obesity*, *20*(12), 2406-2411; Xu, W. L., Atti, A. R., Gatz, M., Pedersen, N. L., Johansson, B., & Fratiglioni, L. (2011). Midlife overweight and obesity increase late-life dementia risk A population-based twin study. *Neurology*, 76(18), 1568-1574.

many emotional, psychosomatic... Hargens, T. A., Kaleth, A. S., Edwards, E. S., & Butner, K. L. (2013). Association between sleep disorders, obesity, and exercise: a review. *Nat Sci Sleep*, 5, 27-35; Eliacik, K., Bolat, N., Koçyiğit, C., Kanik, A., Selkie, E., Yilmaz, H.,... & Dundar, B. N. (2016). Internet addiction, sleep and health-related life quality among obese individuals: a comparison study of the growing problems in adolescent health. *Eating and Weight Disorders-Studies on Anorexia, Bulimia and Obesity*, 21(4), 709-717; Luppino, F. S., de Wit, L. M., Bouvy, P. F., Stijnen, T., Cuijpers, P., Penninx, B. W., & Zitman, F. G. (2010). Overweight, obesity, and depression: a systematic review and meta-analysis of longitudinal studies. *Archives of general psychiatry*, 67(3), 220-229; Gariepy, G., Nitka, D., & Schmitz, N. (2010). The association between obesity and anxiety disorders in the population: a systematic review and meta-analysis. *International journal of obesity*, 34(3), 407-419; Rankin, J., Matthews, L., Cobley, S., Han, A., Sanders, R., Wiltshire, H. D., & Baker, J. S. (2016). Psychological consequences of childhood obesity: psychiatric comorbidity and prevention. *Adolescent Health, Medicine and Therapeutics*, 7, 125; Janssen, I., Craig, W. M., Boyce, W. F., & Pickett, W. (2004). Associations between overweight and obesity with bullying behaviors in school-aged children. *Pediatrics*, 113(5), 1187-1194.

DIETARY RESTRICTION... Johnston, B. C., Kanters, S., Bandayrel, K., Wu, P., Naji, F., Siemieniuk, R. A.,... & Jansen, J. P. (2014). Comparison of weight loss among named diet programs in overweight and obese adults: a meta-analysis. *Jama*, 312(9), 923-933; Miller, W. C., Koceja, D. M., & Hamilton, E. J. (1997). A meta-analysis of the past 25 years of weight loss research using diet, exercise or diet plus exercise intervention. *International journal of obesity*, 21(10), 941-947; Lourida, I., Soni, M., Thompson-Coon, J., Purandare, N., Lang, I. A., Ukoumunne, O. C., & Llewellyn, D. J. (2013). Mediterranean diet, cognitive function, and dementia: a systematic review. *Epidemiology*, 24(4), 479-489; Féart, C., Samieri, C., & Barberger-Gateau, P. (2010). Mediterranean diet and cognitive function in older adults. *Current opinion in clinical nutrition and metabolic care*, 13(1), 14; Serra-Majem, L., Roman, B., & Estruch, R. (2006). Scientific evidence of interventions using the Mediterranean diet: a systematic review. *Nutrition reviews, 64(suppl 1)*, S27-S47.

EXERCISE BRINGS THE LOST COGNITIVE FUNCTIONS BACK... Napoli, N., Shah, K., Waters, D. L., Sinacore, D. R., Qualls, C., & Villareal, D. T. (2014). Effect of weight loss, exercise, or both on cognition and quality of life in obese older adults. *The American journal of clinical nutrition*, 100(1), 189-198; Chen, S.R., Tseng, C.L., Kuo, S.Y. and Chang, Y.K., (2016). Effects of a physical activity intervention on autonomic and executive functions in obese young adolescents: A randomized controlled trial. *Health Psychology*, 35(10), 1120; Davis, C. L., Tomporowski, P. D., McDowell, J. E., Austin, B. P., Miller, P. H., Yanasak, N. E.,... & Naglieri, J. A. (2011). Exercise improves executive function and achievement and alters brain activation in overweight children: a randomized, controlled trial. *Health Psychology, 30*(1), 91; Crova, C., Struzzolino, I., Marchetti, R., Masci, I., Vannozzi, G., Forte, R., & Pesce, C. (2014). Cognitively challenging physical activity benefits executive function in overweight children. *Journal of sports sciences*, 32(3), 201-211; Krafft, C. E., Schaeffer, D. J., Schwarz, N. F., Chi, L., Weinberger, A. L., Pierce, J. E.,... & Davis, C. L. (2014). Improved frontoparietal white matter integrity in overweight children is associated with attendance at an after-school exercise program. *Developmental neuroscience*, *36*(1), 1-9; Parikh, T., & Stratton, G. (2011). Influence of intensity of physical activity on adiposity and cardiorespiratory fitness in 5–18 year olds. *Sports Medicine*, *41*(6), 477-488.

EXERCISE PROMOTES HEALTHY DIET... Teixeira, P. J., Carraça, E. V., Marques, M. M., Rutter, H., Oppert, J. M., De Bourdeaudhuij, I.,... & Brug, J. (2015). Successful behavior change in obesity interventions in adults: a systematic review of self-regulation mediators. *BMC medicine*, 13(1), 1; Groppe, K., & Elsner, B. (2015). Executive function and weight status in children: A one-year longitudinal perspective. *Child Neuropsychology*, 1-19; Groppe, K., & Elsner, B. (2015). The influence of hot and cool executive function on the development of eating styles related to overweight in children. *Appetite*, 87, 127-136.

Many factors such as stress... Hewagalamulage, S. D., Lee, T. K., Clarke, I. J., & Henry, B. A. (2016). Stress, cortisol, and obesity: a role for cortisol responsiveness in identifying individuals prone to obesity. *Domestic Animal Endocrinology*; Sominsky, L., & Spencer, S. J. (2014). Eating behavior and stress: a pathway to obesity. *Frontiers in psychology*, 5, 434; Luppino, F. S., de Wit, L. M., Bouvy, P. F., Stijnen, T., Cuijpers, P., Penninx, B. W., & Zitman, F. G. (2010). Overweight, obesity, and depression: a systematic review and meta-analysis of longitudinal studies. *Archives of general psychiatry*, 67(3), 220-229; Schuch, F., Vancampfort, D., Firth, J., Rosenbaum, S., Ward, P., Reichert, T.,... & Stubbs, B. (2016). Physical activity and sedentary behavior in people with major depressive disorder: A systematic review and meta-analysis. *Journal of Affective Disorders*; Lee, S. H., Paz-Filho, G., Mastronardi, C., Licinio, J., & Wong, M. L. (2016). Is increased antidepressant exposure a contributory factor to the obesity pandemic? *Translational psychiatry*, 6(3), e759; Gangwisch, J. E., Malaspina, D., Boden-Albala, B., & Heymsfield, S. B. (2005). Inadequate sleep as a risk factor for obesity: analyses of the NHANES I. SLEEP-NEW YORK THEN WESTCHESTER-, 28(10), 1289; Fatima, Y.,

& Mamun, A. A. (2016). Sleep quality and obesity in young subjects: a meta-analysis. *Obesity Reviews*, 17(11), 1154-1166.

144

INDEX

ABOUT THE AUTHOR

Chong Chen is a research scientist at the RIKEN Brain Science Institute in Wako, a suburb of Tokyo, Japan. He studied at Hokkaido University, where he obtained a Ph.D. in Medicine and won several academic awards, including the Takakuwa Eimatsu Award.

Chong has been the author of some 20 articles, all of which have been published in professional journals and which cover several aspects of his fields of expertise; neuroscience, psychiatry and psychology.

In addition to these important pieces, Chong has now written two books. **Fitness Powered Brains: Optimize Your Productivity, Leadership and Performance,** is exactly what it sounds like and is ideal for business people, while **Plato's Insight: How Physical Exercise Boosts Mental Excellence** shows how being physically active can directly correlate to mental ability and how this fact has been known for centuries. In fact, one of Plato's quotations was part of the inspiration for the title – *"with education and exercise, man can attain perfection."*

When he has free time, Chong likes to get some fresh air and exercise by cycling. He also loves playing ping-pong, reads novels and poems and is a huge fan of the Argentine Tango.

As far as the future goes, Chong hopes that he will be able to translate scientific findings into ways that will allow regular people to live better lives. And through his books, he hopes that he can reach a much wider audience.

You can contact Chong Chen and follow what he is writing about at:

https://brainandlife.net

Twitter: @ChongChenBlog

Email: chen@brainandlife.net

www.ingramcontent.com/pod-product-compliance
Lightning Source LLC
Chambersburg PA
CBHW022055050726
47591CB00002B/550